EXPLAINING READING

Explaining
READING

A Resource for Explicit Teaching of the Common Core Standards

THIRD EDITION

Gerald G. Duffy

THE GUILFORD PRESS
New York   London

© 2014 The Guilford Press
A Division of Guilford Publications, Inc.
72 Spring Street, New York, NY 10012
www.guilford.com

Printed in the United States of America

This book is printed on acid-free paper.

Last digit is print number: 9   8   7   6   5   4   3   2   1

Library of Congress Cataloging-in-Publication Data

Duffy, Gerald G.
    Explaining reading : a resource for explicit teaching of the common core
standards / Gerald G. Duffy. — Third edition.
        pages cm
    Includes index.
    ISBN 978-1-4625-1556-1 (paperback)—ISBN 978-1-4625-1582-0 (cloth)
    1. Reading. 2. Reading—Remedial teaching. 3. Vocabulary. I. Title.
LB1050.42.D84 2014
372.4—dc23

                                                                    2008021106

To Auleen

About the Author

Gerald G. Duffy, EdD, is the former William Moran Distinguished Professor of Literacy and Reading at the University of North Carolina at Greensboro and Professor Emeritus at Michigan State University. Now retired and living in Deer Park, Washington, he was an elementary and middle school teacher, researcher, and teacher educator for over 50 years. His teaching and research focused on the explicit teaching of reading, on comprehension, and on the development of adaptive teachers. A past president of the National Reading Conference (now the Literacy Research Association) and a member of the Reading Hall of Fame, Dr. Duffy has worked with teachers and children across the United States and overseas. He has written and edited several books on reading instruction and has published over 150 articles and research studies.

Preface

This is the third edition of *Explaining Reading*. Like the first two editions, it is written for classroom teachers faced with teaching reading skills and strategies to struggling readers. Unlike the previous editions, however, this edition is organized around the Common Core State Standards for English Language Arts.* Consequently, the book's subtitle has been changed to reflect this new emphasis, and the teaching examples are now arranged to match the Common Core's structure.

There are several reasons why I have based the third edition on the Common Core reading standards. First, teachers are to be held accountable for meeting these standards and, therefore, will need help in responding to this new challenge. Second, in analyzing the Common Core, I found nothing wrong with what it says students should learn, and I would teach each of the listed standards. Furthermore, the Common Core's emphasis on "reading for purpose and understanding" reflects my personal commitment to engaging readers in authentic tasks.

Nonetheless, my decision to revise this edition in accordance with the Common Core was not an easy one. Like many other educators, I worry about the Common Core's expectation that every student will achieve every standard at the same time; that corporate America may translate standards into rigid, scripted commercial programs; and that the high-stakes testing abuses we have recently experienced will be repeated.

---

*Common Core State Standards Initiative (National Governors Association Center for Best Practices and Council of Chief State School Officers, 2010). Available at *www.corestandards.org*.

Despite these concerns, I based this edition on the Common Core not only for the reasons already stated, but also because in the end I believe the Common Core can be implemented while still promoting teachers' professional autonomy, differentiated instruction, and the engagement of students in sensible and worthwhile literacy tasks.

Consequently, this edition of *Explaining Reading* is more than a practical resource for teaching the Common Core standards. Although I do hope it helps your students meet those standards, my major goal is to help you implement the Common Core in ways that encourage adaptive, differentiated, and creative (as well as explicit) instruction.

Acknowledgments

I gratefully acknowledge the following educators for their thoughtful and conscientious reading of early versions of this edition of *Explaining Reading:* Drs. Seth Parsons, Kelly Puzio, Dena Reems, and Margaret Vaughn; Lydia Fesler, the retired director of literacy for a large urban school district; and classroom teachers Stephanie Bradshaw, Chris Cahoon, George Conger, Jessica Dahlin, Mari Harris, Thomas Kuhns, Terri Christie-Lutes, Lynette Rose, Amy Wise, and Kim Yearsley. Their suggestions significantly improved the book.

I owe a special thank-you to Liona Lutes, whose patience and expertise with technology were instrumental in the preparation of several teaching examples.

Contents

PART I
INTRODUCTION

Chapter 1

Five Foundational Principles

Explaining Reading provides 30 sample lessons you can adapt for use when preparing students to meet the Common Core State Standards for reading in grades K–8. It is divided into two parts: Part I consists of five introductory chapters; Part II consists of the 30 teaching examples.

The book is governed by five foundational principles.

- First, examples are keyed to the Common Core State Standards for English Language Arts because the Common Core will drive reading assessment for the foreseeable future.
- Second, each teaching example illustrates how to explicitly explain a particular type of Common Core reading standard because research has established the effectiveness of explicit explanations, especially with struggling readers.
- Third, every teaching example is embedded in an authentic literacy task because we want students to experience reading as worthwhile and useful.
- Fourth, teacher professionalism is emphasized because each teaching example is hypothetical and must be thoughtfully adapted.
- Finally, a literate classroom environment is assumed because explicit teaching is most successful when embedded within an enticing setting.

THE FIRST FOUNDATION: THE COMMON CORE

The Common Core State Standards represent the most recent evolution in a longstanding national effort to improve classroom instruction. For instance, the reading standards reflect such recent insights about how to improve literacy instruction as:

- Emphasis should be on building knowledge throughout the grades.
- Comprehension should be emphasized.
- Information text should be emphasized as much as narrative text.
- Close reading of complex text, with a focus on analysis and evaluation in a variety of content areas should be emphasized.
- A major instructional goal should be reading for purpose and understanding.

These insights represent a shift in emphasis, not a major change. We have long understood the need to emphasize comprehension; to feature expository text as well as narrative text; to develop higher order thinking such as analyzing and evaluating; and to ensure that reading skills and strategies are not taught in isolation. What the Common Core does is make these things official.

It does so by specifying benchmarks for student assessment, which means that teacher accountability will be based, at least in part, on how well students perform on tests of these standards. But missing from the Common Core is what teachers should do if students cannot meet a particular standard. This book meets that need.

The book's mission is to describe for each type of Common Core standard (1) how to determine whether students are ready to meet a standard and (2) if they are not, how to explain the standard explicitly. To make the book as useful as possible, the Part II examples match the order and organization of the Common Core (see also Chapter 4).

> Be cautioned, however: The book follows the order in which standards are listed in the Common Core and is not intended for use as a sequential reading curriculum or as a reading program to be followed in order.

THE SECOND FOUNDATION: EXPLICIT EXPLANATIONS

All the sample lessons in Part II illustrate how to provide explicit explanations. An explicit explanation is a set of verbal statements describing how to do a particular reading skill or strategy or standard. The goal is to make visible for students the invisible mental processing good readers use when they read. When students struggle to meet one or another skill, or strategy, or standard, explicit explanations "demystify" what for them is a mystifying task.

We do not employ explanations routinely; we employ them only when students are struggling. You do not need a formal test to assess whether students are struggling. Informal "kid watching" is quite adequate. Each Part II example provides suggestions for what to watch for to assess whether students are ready to meet a particular type of Common Core reading standard.

When we notice that students are *not* ready to meet a standard, it is time to say, "Let me show you how to do it." This "showing how" includes:

- A clear statement of what is to be learned and why it is important (the objective).
- A statement about what students must particularly pay attention to (the secret).
- A verbal description of the thinking involved in doing the skill or strategy (modeling the thinking).
- Gradually reduced amounts of assistance (scaffolded assistance).
- Continued applications to reading.

Chapter 4, as well as each Part II example, describes each of the above components in detail. The goal is to help you provide students with explicit information about the mental processing involved and to help you guide their learning through scaffolding and application.

This book is useful because when students do not meet a standard you will need to teach them how to do it. That is, you must describe the mental processing involved. As veteran readers, we are seldom conscious of the mental processing we employ as we read, so it is difficult to come up with an explicit explanation on our own. Part II helps with this problem by providing a "starter" you can adapt when faced with the task of explaining how to meet a particular standard.

Explicit explanations are effective, but they are not magic. The poverty and family difficulties often associated with struggling readers will still make instruction difficult. In the end, what makes the difference is creative and patient teachers who insist that all students can learn to read and who are relentless in providing explicit help.

THE THIRD FOUNDATION:
BALANCING STANDARDS WITH "REAL" READING

Standards are helpful benchmarks. But when they focus only on skills and strategies, students think reading is a narrow, isolated task. The Common Core itself recognizes this problem and tries to counter it by making "reading for purpose and understanding" a separate standard under the heading of "Range of Reading and Level of Text Complexity" (Standard 10). Because of the central importance of this standard, I have not provided a single teaching example to explain it. Instead, each Part II teaching example is situated "inside" a motivating task that focuses on reading for purpose and understanding.

An Example of Teaching "Inside" a Larger Task

Consider the following example of a second-grade teacher. Consistent with the Common Core standard for Informational Text (*RI.2.5: Know and use various text features (e.g., captions, bold print, subheadings, glossaries, indexes, electronic menus, icons) to locate key facts or information in a text efficiently)*, she must teach her students what an index is and how to use it. She could simply provide an explicit explanation of how to use an index and then give them a worksheet for practice. But she does not do that. She wants her students to see that indexes are useful when they are doing purposeful reading tasks. Consequently, she uses students' concern about new animal control laws passed by the township and suggests writing to the town council to influence how the new laws are being enforced. In preparation, she suggests informational text for her students to read. But in the midst of doing that reading—that is, *inside* the larger activity of searching for information useful in influencing the town council—the teacher provides explicit instruction about how to use an index. By first involving students in a purposeful reading task and then teaching them how to use indexes *inside* that task, she accomplishes three goals: She motivates students by engaging them in reading they see as purposeful, she teaches indexes as a practical and immediately useful tool for accomplishing that task, and she gives students experiences that help them learn to value reading.

The "reading for purpose and understanding" standard is crucial because "what they *do* is what they think it is." That is, if students do skill sheets most of the time, they tend to think reading is skills; if they read for authentic purposes much of the time, they tend to think reading is for enrichment and empowerment. We must provide them with experiences that cause them to draw the latter conclusion.

As with the "starter" modeling and scaffolding provided for each example in Part II, the "real reading" tasks in each example cannot be used exactly as written. I invented them to illustrate what *could* be done; your situation will be different, so you must create your own "reading for purpose and understanding" tasks for your students. While none of us are creative enough to come up with the perfect motivating task every time, we can all try to ensure that instruction in Common Core standards does not begin and end with skill sheets, practice exercises, and tests. Whatever you can do to help students see reading as purposeful is better than focusing exclusively on skills and testing.

The Game at the End of the Week

We can better understand why reading for "purpose and understanding" is motivating if we consider a sports analogy. For instance, kids love to play baseball. They will practice skills such as fielding ground balls for hours without complaint. Why? Because there is a game at the end of the week. That is, they are learning to field ground balls *inside* a larger and (to them) more important task—that of playing the game at the end of the week. Students can be equally motivated to meet Common Core standards or to learn reading skills and strategies if they see that the standards or skills or strategies are going to be used to do something important and are not just isolated things learned to pass a test.

THE FOURTH FOUNDATION: ADAPTIVE TEACHERS

This book is a practical tool and a useful resource. However, it does not eliminate the difficulties of teaching or the need for professional thought.

For instance, the Common Core expects every student to meet every standard on an arbitrary schedule. But every teacher knows that kids learn in different ways and on different schedules. Individual student differences require teachers to be creative in orchestrating lessons so that each student learns what is needed when it is needed. Such differentiation of instruction will continue to be required when using this book.

Also, while the 30 examples in Part II appear to be packaged lessons, they cannot be used that way. They are all hypothetical situations. None will be an exact fit for your students or your teaching situation. You will have to invent your own authentic reading tasks, and you will have to adjust every suggested explanation to fit your situation.

Scaffolding students' understandings will especially require thinking on your feet. No matter how well you plan, students do not always understand explanations in the way you expected. Responding on-the-fly is essential.

And to make it even more difficult, you must be thoughtfully adaptive in a world that today seems to discourage thoughtful teaching. Recent federal and state pressures, directives, mandates, and assessments, as well as highly prescriptive commercial reading programs, seem designed to limit teacher decision making and creativity.

But this book is not for teachers who want to avoid making decisions or being creative. To the contrary, it assumes that the hallmarks of exciting and effective classroom teaching is teacher adaptation and creativity, and that scripts and highly prescriptive instructional programs make for boring instruction. Consequently, while the 30 examples in Part II may appear to be prescriptive, they are just a framework. For them to be effective, you must view each as merely a "starter" or a guide you can use to make your own assessment decisions, to create your own authentic literacy tasks, and to create your own explanations.

THE FIFTH FOUNDATION: A LITERATE ENVIRONMENT

Skill and strategy instruction is most effective, and standards are more easily met when the classroom context invites students to engage in literate activity. While Part II of this book is dedicated to explicit explanations of Common Core reading standards, explicit explanation is only one part of a good reading program. For explanations to be most effective, they must occur in a classroom that invites literate activity. The following six suggestions are illustrative:

1. *Create a text-rich environment.* If exciting and interesting texts are available in the classroom, students are more likely to read. Consequently, students should have access to a wide range of high-quality trade books, both narrative and informational. The usual guideline is at least 30 trade books per student, including a wide range of genres and levels of difficulty attractively arranged to encourage browsing. The environment might include beanbag chairs or rocking chairs in an area where trade books are displayed to further entice kids to read. Additionally,

there should be lots of non-book texts, including maps, globes, computers, student-generated texts, and charts produced by both teachers and students, and magazines and newspapers.

2. *Do daily read-alouds.* There are many benefits when teachers read stories and informational text to their classes. The most important one is that it models the teacher's own love of and commitment to reading. Reading aloud also acquaints children with different kinds of text and provides them with background knowledge they might not otherwise encounter on their own. And, finally, read-alouds are relaxing times. The implicit message is that reading can be fun. As such, it sends an important message and is an important instructional support.

3. *Ensure that students have lots of time to read.* Free reading is sometimes squeezed out of today's classrooms by the pressure to prepare for tests. That is a mistake. You cannot learn to do anything unless you do it a lot and have some choice about it. This principle is as true for learning to read as for anything else. Students cannot become enthusiastic readers unless they read a lot and can choose the books they want to read on their own. The general guideline is that students should do 45–60 minutes of free-choice reading a day. The time can be broken up, with 15 minutes during a designated free reading time, 7 minutes during a break in activities, and so on. But the bottom line is that they probably will not become enthusiastic readers unless they can read lots of books that excite them.

Focus on Connected Text

Most of the reading students do should be connected text. *Connected text* is text that contains a coherent message. A story is an example of connected text; a chapter in a social studies textbook is connected text; a newspaper article is connected text; graphic novels are connected text. However, fill-in-the-blank worksheets or word lists are not connected text. Students become readers by reading connected text.

---

4. *Make knowledge building a priority.* Knowledge depends on the experiences you have. The more experiences you have, the more words you know; the more words you know, the more knowledge you have, and the better you read. Consequently, it is crucial to build knowledge. Content areas such as social studies and science are the best sources of new experiences, new knowledge, and new vocabulary, and they should be an integral part of a literate environment.

5. *Integrate writing into your reading instruction.* Writing and reading are mutually supportive. The more students write, the better they read; the more they read, the better they write. Consequently, writing in journals, writing stories, writing letters, writing notes to friends or family, and writing informational text in support of a class project all support the development of reading skill. For that reason, each Part II example provides a suggestion for linking that Common Core reading standard to a Common Core writing standard. As much as possible, Common Core reading standards should be taught together with or linked to Common Core writing standards.

6. *Conversation is important.* Just as reading and writing are mutually supportive, reading and oral language are mutually supportive. Discussion in which students have a voice and an active role is best, while traditional question-and-answer formats in which students are put in a passive position are less effective. To be most effective, classroom talk should be collaborative rather than submissive, active rather than passive, and conversational rather than interrogative.

SUMMARY

This edition of *Explaining Reading* is organized to match the Common Core's structure. It provides an example of how to explain each type of Common Core standard, and it reflects the Common Core emphasis on reading for purpose and understanding. It is designed with struggling readers in mind. While some students will not need explicit explanations, others will struggle to meet Common Core standards. The resources of this book are provided for these students.

But this book also has another purpose. While explicit explanations are featured, the undergirding argument is that the Common Core standards are not enough by themselves. Also needed are adaptive, thoughtful teachers who value differentiated instruction, who creatively use instructional resources within a larger literate context, and who understand that standards are merely steppingstones to the ultimate goal of reading instruction—students who value reading as an important part of their lives.

Chapter 2

How Comprehension and Foundational Skills Work

The Common Core State Standards for English Language Arts lists three categories of reading standards:

1. Reading: Literature.
2. Reading: Informational Text.
3. Reading: Foundational Skills.

The literature and informational text standards focus on comprehension; the foundational skills standards focus on identifying words and on fluency. Collectively, the standards specify acceptable performance in comprehension, word identification, and fluency at various grade levels. For instance, by grade 2 students should be able to answer questions about key details in both literature and informational text, to decode multisyllable words, and to read grade-level texts for purpose and understanding (listed by the Common Core in a category called "Range of Reading and Level of Complexity").

Some students will meet these benchmarks with little assistance; others will not. You will need to teach those students who do not. In order to do so, you need to understand how comprehension, word identification, and fluency work. This chapter provides that background.

Skill or Strategy?

What is a skill and what is a strategy? A *skill* is something you do without thinking about it. You do it the same way every time. Tying your shoes is an example of a skill. Instantly recognizing and saying a word such as *the* is an example of a reading skill. You do these things without thinking about them. They are automatized. A *strategy*, in contrast, is a plan. You must reason when you do it, and you often adjust the plan as you go along. Planning a trip by car is strategic. You are thoughtful, making decisions about what highways to take, where to spend the night, and so on. And if you run into unanticipated problems along the way (such as extensive road construction), you adjust your strategy—you change your route. Similarly, reading strategies require readers to make thoughtful use of clues and prior knowledge, and require a readiness to change or adjust when subsequent text clues provide more information

HOW COMPREHENSION WORKS

Comprehension is the essence of reading. If we do not understand a text's message, we are not reading.

The Common Core divides comprehension into literature standards and informational text standards. It makes this distinction to emphasize that informational text should receive just as much emphasis as literature. But they also do so because there are features that distinguish literature from informational text. For instance, literature is distinguished by its text types (see Example 6 in Part II), by its text structure (see Example 7 in Part II), by its use of nonliteral language (see Example 5 in Part II), and by its use of illustrations (see Example 9 in Part II); informational text is distinguished by text features (see Example 15 in Part II), by text structure (see Example 16 in Part II), and by the use of graphic information such as tables and charts (see Example 18 in Part II).

But despite these differences, when it comes to the act of comprehending, the thinking process is basically the same for both literature and informational text. Both require vocabulary knowledge and a strategic thinking process.

The Role of Vocabulary

Vocabulary is fundamentally important because reading comprehension depends on prior knowledge or knowledge about the world. You cannot comprehend something for which you have no prior knowledge. Prior knowledge is reflected in the words we know. If we have knowledge about something, it means we have words to describe that "something." When comprehending, readers say to themselves, in effect, "I have prior knowledge about the words on this page, so I think the author must mean something close to what I've experienced relative to these words." In short, readers use their past experiences with the words in the text to build a meaning that is consistent with their experiences with these words.

When Should We Start Teaching Vocabulary and Comprehension?

It is often assumed that vocabulary and comprehension should be delayed until after students have learned how to decode. Not so. If we teach vocabulary and comprehension in listening situations, instruction can be started as early as preschool. Comprehending oral messages requires the same strategies as comprehending printed messages, so the earlier we start emphasizing vocabulary and comprehension in listening situations, the more likely it is that students will learn to comprehend. The Common Core recognizes this fact, and makes the point by listing comprehension of literature and information text first ahead of foundational skills.

When you don't know the meaning of a word, it means you do not have background knowledge or have not had experiences in that area. Without background knowledge—that is, without the vocabulary that comes with experiences—there is no comprehension.

An Example of How Experience Works

As schoolteachers, most of us have difficulty comprehending texts on nuclear reactors. We do not have much prior knowledge about nuclear reactors, so we do not know the meaning of the words used to describe them. Physicists, in contrast, have experience with nuclear physics, know those words, and can construct subtle and complex meaning. Similarly, students who have always lived in New York City have little prior knowledge about buttes and mesas—that is, they do not have meaning for those words—so they would have more difficulty constructing meaning for a text about the desert Southwest; in contrast, children from Phoenix would find it easier because they have experienced "buttes" and "mesas" and therefore know what those words mean.

In short, you cannot comprehend unless you have experienced something and learned the words associated with it. So vocabulary instruction is crucial.

The best way to increase vocabulary is by immersing students in written and oral language. Given a rich language background at home, immersion in substantive subject-matter knowledge in school, and lots of experiences with new concepts and ideas, vocabulary often develops "naturally" with no intentional instruction. But when those conditions are not present, vocabularies may be inadequate. In those cases, teachers must provide intentional vocabulary instruction.

New vocabulary can be developed intentionally through direct experience, as when students visit a farm and learn new words about farms and farm animals, or they can be learned through vicarious experience, as when one reads about farms and farm animals or hears about them in a video or on TV. Teaching word meaning in school is also a vicarious experience under most circumstances in that the concept cannot be directly experienced but must be talked about or viewed in an illustration.

In school, most new word meanings are learned because teachers directly teach the meanings of new words. Some teachers teach vocabulary by providing definitions, often through dictionary work. However, this seldom works. Students may memorize a word and its definition, but they almost always forget it.

A better teaching method is to intentionally and directly teach each week the meanings of 10 to 15 words students will be reading and using that week. Normally, it is best to draw the new words from content areas such as social studies and science because those areas involve new knowledge students have not previously experienced. Example 13 in Part II is an example of how to directly teach a word meaning; Example 5 in Part II is an example of how to teach meanings of descriptive words used in literature.

How Important Is Prior Knowledge?

It has been estimated that as much as 50–60% of successful comprehension is tied to background knowledge. Knowing something about a topic before one begins to read—that is, knowing the meaning of the words used—is crucial to being able to construct meaning from a text.

In addition to intentionally and directly teaching 10–15 new words weekly, we should also teach students to use strategies to figure out word meanings they encounter when reading on their own. Many of the new words students learn are encountered during independent reading. By teaching strategies for figuring out unknown words as they read, students can learn more than just the 10–15 weekly words. See Example 14 in Part II for an example of how to teach figuring out words using context.

Comprehension: A Strategic Process

Comprehension is strategic. If we have prior knowledge about a topic in a text, we can use strategies—or plans—to construct meaning based on our experience, and we can adjust and change those plans as we go along. The following box illustrates some of the distinguishing characteristics of comprehension. I invented this example to demonstrate that comprehension is a continuous process of using text clues—mainly word meanings but also syntactic clues—to access relevant categories of prior knowledge and, on the basis of our own experiences with those categories of knowledge, making predictions about what meaning is to come. Because good readers change their predictions as they proceed, I also invented subsequent text clues that would cause us to access different categories of knowledge and to either abandon or adjust a first prediction in favor of a new or modified prediction that fits the new information. Hopefully, the example illustrates that comprehension is a fluid cycle of predicting–monitoring–repredicting; that is, readers use prior knowledge to predict what meaning is coming, monitor during reading to see what does come next, and revise the prediction when an anticipated meaning does not pan out. This predicting–monitoring–repredicting cycle is fundamental to all comprehension.

An Example of How Comprehension Works

To illustrate how comprehension works, let's try to comprehend a bit of text, piece by piece. We look first at the title. It says "The Unanticipated Destination." As soon as we see that, our minds begin to generate hypotheses, or predictions. We begin to activate our own experiences about trips and about starting out to go to one place but then ending up in another. Assuming we all have similar background experiences, we anticipate that this is a story about a trip, and we get ready for that meaning.

Then we look at the first line of the selection. It says, "I flew into GEG." Several things happen at once. You look at the word *flew* and access the "flying" category in your mind. While you may have originally

---

been thinking of a trip by car, you now dump that image and replace it with an image of airplanes (again, if your background experiences are different, you might generate a different image). If you have experienced flying commercially, you probably think about a large jet airplane, and you see an image in your mind of rows of people sitting in the coach section (teachers seldom create an image of the first-class section since few of us have had experience sitting in first class). If you have never flown commercially, however, your image of what it looks like inside an airplane will be limited to what you have experienced in movies or in magazines and, as such, will probably be less detailed. And while you may use the syntactic clue "into" to figure out that "GEG" must be a place, you will probably be mystified as to exactly what that place is (unless, of course, you fly a lot and have lots of experience finding your baggage, in which case you have already figured out that GEG is an airport identifier, and that, therefore, GEG is an airport. You may even know that GEG is the Spokane, Washington, airport if your experiences include travel to the Northwest).

Now let's look at the next line of the selection. It says, "But they wouldn't let me land." If up until now we had pictured people sitting in the coach section of a large jet airplane, that image is now replaced by the image of a pilot in the cockpit of an airplane. Our experience tells us that if the passenger image had been correct, the sentence would have said, "But they wouldn't let *us* land." It is only the pilot who says "They wouldn't let *me* land." So we change our prediction. We begin thinking about pilots, not passengers.

So, we say comprehension is:

- Proactive, because a reader must be actively thinking and constantly monitoring the meaning.
- Tentative, because predictions made in one moment may change in the next moment.
- Personal, in that meaning resides in the reader's interpretation, which in turn is controlled by his or her prior knowledge.
- Transactive, because the reader's background interacts with the author's intention.
- Thoughtful, because you must always analyze the clues the author provides.
- Imagistic, because (in literature particularly) you use the author's

descriptive language to create a picture in your mind of what is happening.

- Inferential, because the reader can only make a calculated guess about the author's meaning since the author was operating from one set of experiences and the reader from another.
- Reflective, in that good readers monitor their predictions and change them when needed.
- Evaluative, in that good readers evaluate what they have read and determine its significance and/or how it can be used after finishing reading.

Although readers use only a few strategies, they use them in various combinations over and over again, with slight variation from one reading situation to another. These strategies include:

Making predictions.
Monitoring and questioning what is happening.
Adjusting and/or changing predictions as you go.
Creating images in the mind.
Reflecting on and analyzing the significance, importance, or validity of what has been read.

These strategies are often employed in stages:

Before you begin reading.
As you begin reading.
During reading.
After reading.

Before-You-Begin Strategies

Readers are more motivated, and comprehend more, when they have a purpose for reading. So the best comprehension begins before reading when the reader asks, "Why am I reading this?" "How will I use it?" Even if the text is a story being read just for enjoyment, the purpose should be clear to the reader. Because of its fundamental importance, each Part II teaching example begins with an "Introducing the Lesson" section that makes clear to students why they are reading a particular text.

As-You-Begin Strategies

Predicting is the strategy relied upon most as you begin. As soon as a reader sees the title of a selection or looks at a picture on a cover or reads a first line, prior knowledge is triggered and, on the basis of that prior knowledge, predictions (or hypotheses) are formed about what is to come. Predictions can be based on three kinds of prior knowledge.

First, predictions can be based on *prior knowledge about the purpose of the reading*. As noted previously, a crucial before-you-read question is, "Why am I reading this?" It is crucial in terms of motivation (students are more likely to be engaged if the task is worth the effort). But purpose is also important because it can suggest what one looks for when reading, or what predictions to make. For instance, when the purpose is to find out the score of last night's game when reading the sports page of the morning paper, a reader will note only the score of the game but not the details. In contrast, when the purpose is to bake a cake with a recipe, predictions focus on details because those details are crucial to cooking tasks.

Second, predictions can be based on *prior knowledge about the topic*. For instance, if a reader picks up a book with a picture of an elephant on the cover, or if one of the first sentences is about elephants, it is anticipated that something will be learned about elephants, and the reader uses what is known about elephants to make predictions about what is coming.

Third, predictions can be based on *prior knowledge about type of text*. Recognizing the text as a narrative, for example, triggers prior knowledge about story structure, and we predict we will learn in the first few pages about a setting, a character, and a problem the character is facing. Recognizing a text as informational, in contrast, triggers prior knowledge about fact books and information, and we predict we will learn factual information.

During-Reading Strategies

The primary strategy used during reading is the predicting–monitoring–repredicting cycle. Successful readers pay attention to what is happening and anticipate that there might be a need to change a prediction. It is as if readers are constantly engaged in silent questioning, saying to themselves as they read along, "Does this fit what I expected? Does this fit what I expected? Does this fit what I expected?" When a reader answers by saying, "No, this no longer fits the prediction I made," then a new prediction must be made.

The predicting–monitoring–repredicting cycle is repeated over and over again as the reader proceeds through text. It is not a static, one-time process. It is a process that goes on constantly. As readers become proficient, they no longer see three individual strategies; they see a single process of predicting–monitoring–repredicting (e.g., see Examples 1 and 11 in Part II).

While the predicting–monitoring–repredicting cycle is the dominant during-reading strategy, readers sometimes use other strategies. For instance, when encountering descriptive language in literature, good comprehenders may use their prior knowledge to create images—that is, to infer what the scene in the narrative looks like or feels like (e.g., see Examples 2 and 5 in Part II).

All Comprehension Requires Inferences

Inferring (or "reading between the lines") is often taught as a separate strategy (see Example 2 in Part II). In fact, however, all reading comprehension requires the reader to make inferences. When a reader makes a prediction, he or she uses background knowledge to "infer" what will come next. We call it "predicting," but predicting is an inference. Even answering a literal question requires inferring (if a text says "The girl wore her "best dress," the reader infers, based on his or her personal experience, what a "best dress" looks like). Because comprehenders always use their own background knowledge to construct meaning, they are always making strategic and logical guesses about what the author intends. That is, they are inferring the author's meaning.

In summary, the most important during-reading strategy is the predict–monitor–repredict cycle. As noted earlier, comprehension involves the use of relatively few strategies that are applied in a variety of different situations. For instance, the combined predicting–monitoring–repredicting strategy is applied in almost all comprehension examples in Part II.

After-Reading Strategies

Comprehension does not stop when the last page of a selection is read. Good readers reflect after they read. While the depth of reflection and the wording of their questioning vary with grade level, students at all grade levels ask themselves questions that go something like the following:

"Did I achieve the purpose I had for reading this selection?"
"Did I find out what I wanted to find out?"
"How has my thinking changed as a result of the reading I just did?"
"Is what I found out important or accurate?"
"How can I use what I read?"

The following are important after-reading strategies:

Deciding on the main idea in informational text (see Example 11 in Part II) or theme in literature (see Example 3 in Part II).
Drawing conclusions about how characters react (see Example 4 in Part II) or about comparing and contrasting (see Example 10 in Part II) or about point of view (see Example 8 in Part II).
Analyzing positions and views (see Example 17 in Part II).
Evaluating (see Example 19 in Part II).
Synthesizing (see Example 20 in Part II).

A Cautionary Note: Close Reading

While comprehension is a proactive process in which one's personal background experience is used to do the predicting–monitoring–repredicting at the heart of comprehension, the process cannot be random or superficial. Because in the past students have been using background knowledge in less than thoughtful ways in some classrooms, the Common Core emphasizes the need for "close reading." Close reading is often a "during" or "after-reading" task involving analysis and evaluation. It often requires thoughtful, analytical employment of the predicting–monitoring–repredicting process. Just making a random prediction is not enough; there must be careful reasoning based on what the text offers as clues and on prior knowledge. The meaning constructed must reflect the meanings of individual words and must fit the general context of the text's message. The goal of close reading is to promote a more thorough, methodical reading and rereading of text as a means of obtaining deeper understanding. See Examples 17 and 19 in Part II for illustrations of how to teach "close reading."

Summarizing Comprehension

Comprehension is difficult to teach because the process is fluid. We cannot proceduralize comprehension or teach comprehension "rules" because:

1. Different readers have different background experiences and construct different meanings.
2. Readers must adapt comprehension strategies to many different kinds of text situations.
3. Successful readers seldom implement a strategy separately but instead combine several strategies.

Avoiding Rigidity

Describing comprehension strategies as "before," "during," and "after" strategies is a helpful organizational structure for students because it emphasizes the ongoing continuous pursuit of meaning from before starting until well after the last page has been turned. However, the categories are not rigid. Good readers often combine them and use them throughout the reading process. For instance, a good reader may decide on the main idea and make evaluative judgments during reading rather than "after" reading. The important point about presenting comprehension as stages (before, as you begin, during, and after) is that it communicates to students the big understanding that comprehension is a continuous process that begins before reading starts and continues after the last page of text has been read.

HOW WORD IDENTIFICATION WORKS

Word identification is decoding the printed squiggles on the page. The Common Core addresses word identification in the Foundational Skills standards and includes the categories of print concepts, phonological awareness, phonics and word recognition, and fluency. For the purposes of this discussion, these foundational skills will be discussed in three categories:

1. Recognizing words at sight.
2. The variety of ways to analyze words for identification.
3. Fluency.

Recognizing Words at Sight

You cannot read smoothly and fluently, in oral or silent reading, if you cannot quickly say the words. Learning sight words is a visual memory task. Good readers memorize words once they have seen them a few times.

Without a large stock of sight words, reading becomes a laborious, slow, and boring task of figuring out word after word.

Sight-Word Recognition versus Phonics

Sight-word recognition should not be confused with phonics. Knowing a word at sight means remembering the word's visual form as a whole. The recognition is instant. There is no "figuring out" involved. Phonics, in contrast, is figuring out a word by sounding out words letter by letter or syllable by syllable. While sight-word recognition is fast, phonics is slow.

Many children come to school with little to prepare them for learning to recognize words at sight. For a 5-year-old, the left-to-right progression of text across the page or the relatively minor differences between a d and a b or between an m and an n just do not seem important. But, of course, they are. To be able to recognize words at sight, they must understand print directionality, note print detail, and see the differences in the visual forms.

Many children develop these skills almost naturally as a result of early writing experiences, so it is important to involve students in writing activities early. But sometimes writing is not enough. Often, we need to be explicit about explaining the directionality of print (see Example 21 in Part II) and what makes a u different from an n or what distinguishes was from saw (see Example 22 in Part II).

Once the above prerequisites are in place, students can begin learning to recognize words at sight. Again, little in the backgrounds of some 5-year-olds prepares them for holding visual forms of words in their memories. They may remember the M in McDonald's, their name, and words such as $dinosaur$ and $elephant$ that have strong meaning for them. But high-utility words in the English language that serve important grammatical functions, such as the, $into$, and $with$, are often much more difficult.

Good adult readers recognize at sight virtually every word they encounter. They accomplish this primarily by doing lots and lots of reading. The more they read, the more words they encounter; the more words they encounter, the more words they remember and recognize instantly. So, one way to develop sight words is to ensure that your students do a lot of reading of easy connected text.

Sometimes, however, students also need explicit instruction in how to remember sight words. Example 27 in Part II provides an example you can use to plan your own explanations of how to remember a word as a sight word.

The most common and highly utilized words in the English language are taught first. Because the word *the* appears so often, we teach it as a sight word almost immediately. Similarly, we emphasize the other crucial "glue" words (such as prepositions) that appear so frequently in English.

Words that cannot be figured out using phonics are also taught as sight words. For instance, words like *come* and *comb* do not follow standard rules of phonics and are taught as sight words.

Gradually, however, virtually all words become sight words. In third-grade social studies, for instance, readers may encounter the word *geography* for the first time. On that first occasion, they may use phonics to slowly figure out what the word is, or they may have the teacher identify it. Similarly, they may have to slowly figure it out the second time they encounter it, and the third time. But by the fourth or fifth time they see *geography*, they should no longer be figuring it out. They just say it because it has now become a sight word.

Analyzing Words

Word analysis is what a reader does when a word must be figured out because it is not recognized at sight. There are three major analysis techniques: (1) phonics, (2) context, and (3) structural analysis. Good readers will often use all three techniques in combination.

Phonics

Phonics is using alphabet letters and their sounds to figure out unknown words, and it is a major way to figure out words that are not recognized at sight. Phonics instruction has four major components: (1) phonological awareness, (2) letter–sound associations, (3) vowel patterns, and (4) syllabication.

Phonological awareness is the ability to hear and discriminate sounds in the mind (see Example 23 in Part II). It is not the same as phonics; it is a prerequisite to phonics. Students will have great difficulty with phonics (i.e., with associating letters with their sounds) if they cannot first discriminate one sound from another. Consequently, *phonological awareness is a "sound-only" skill. Letter names are not used.*

Phonological awareness includes being able to identify rhyming words and to discriminate the beginning and ending sounds of words. For instance, if I say "cat" and "rat," can you tell me if they begin the same or differently? Do they end the same or differently? Students should also be able to segment sounds in words or to stretch out the sounds in a word. For instance, if I say the word *man*, can you segment the individual sounds in the word and say them "stretched out," as in *"m-m-a-a-a-n-n"*? And students should be able to blend sounds or put sounds back together. For instance, if I say *"m-m-a-a-a-n-n"* can you tell me that the word I'm saying is *man*? The Common Core lists each of these tasks as a separate standard. However, the process described in Example 23 in Part II can be adapted and used for each of the other three kinds of phonological awareness.

Many children come to school already possessing highly refined phonological awareness skills. They have played word games, have sung songs, and have listened to poems and stories that have funny sounds in them at home. When children have such experiences in their home life, they come to school with the ability to discriminate one sound from another and to manipulate those sounds in their minds. Those children are ready to learn phonics.

However, not all children have played with sounds. Some come to school without being able to discriminate one sound from another. These children need phonological awareness training.

Once children can discriminate among sounds in their mind, they are ready to learn *letter–sound association*, or what sound goes with what letter (see Example 24 in Part II).

Letter–sound association can be complicated because there are many more sounds than letters in the English language. Vowels and vowel combinations are particularly difficult because a single vowel letter can make different sounds in different words. Consequently, beginning phonics instruction emphasizes consonants first because consonants are the most useful and stable of phonic sounds. They are often the beginning and ending letters in words, and they have relatively few sound variations.

The usual sequence of teaching consonant sounds is:

- Single-consonant sounds.
- Consonant blends (in which two or more consonants are blended together, as in the *bl* in *blend* and the *dr* in *draw*).
- Consonant digraphs (in which two consonants together make a new consonant sound, as in the *sh* in *ship* and the *th* in *think*).

Traditionally, phonics instruction has also emphasized the teaching of vowel sounds, but it is a laborious task, and success is often limited. Recently, there has been a shift away from teaching individual vowel sounds in favor of vowel patterns or "decoding by analogy." That is, many words are made up of consonants combined with common phonograms containing a vowel or vowels (recently, the beginning consonant has been called the "onset," and the vowel pattern or phonogram has been called the "rime"). For instance, the word *cat* consists of the initial consonant (or onset) of *c* and the phonogram (or rime) of *-at*. When we know a word like *cat*, we can figure out other words having the same spelling pattern (or vowel sound), such as *sat, rat, bat,* and *flat*. It is a strategy in which a reader uses known vowel patterns to figure out unknown words having the same pattern (see Example 25 in Part II). It is the most efficient way to teach vowel sounds.

Decoding by analogy can also be used to figure out multisyllable words (see Example 26 in Part II). For instance, a long word such as *envelope* can be figured out if the student knows that every syllable must have a vowel sound and that long words are often composed of common spelling patterns. In envelope, for instance, there is the common spelling pattern *-en* (such as *then*), another having the pattern *-ell* (such as *tell*), and another having the pattern *-ope* (such as *hope*).

Context

Context is a technique in which the meaning around an unknown word is used to make a calculated prediction about what the unknown word could be (see Example 14 in Part II).

If, for instance, a reader encounters the unknown word *umbrella* in the sentence "It was raining, so I put up my ———," it is not necessary to go through the longer process of sounding out the word. Given the structure of the sentence and prior experience with umbrellas, it is obvious what the unknown word is.

Context is a strategy because one must be thoughtful and use prior knowledge to decide what the unknown word is. It is often the preferred way of figuring out an unknown word because it is faster and more efficient than sounding out, especially when context and phonics are used together. For instance, context provides limited help in the sentence "It was raining, so I put *on* my————— ." But if we add a phonic cue, such as the letter *h* in the initial position in the blank, we are more likely to predict the unknown word.

Even beginning readers should be taught to use context. For instance, when kindergartners listen to stories being read to them by their teacher, they can learn to use text meaning to predict what word would fill a particular spot in the text. When students are given lots of experience in listening for and using context clues during prereading listening activities, they find it easier to use the same process in reading later on.

Structural Analysis

Structural analysis is the use of word parts such as root words, compound words, prefixes, suffixes, inflectional endings, and Greek and Latin roots to identify unrecognized words. Linguists call these word parts "morphemes," so structural analysis is sometimes referred to as "morphology" or as "morphemic analysis."

To illustrate how it works, consider an unknown word such as *unhappy*. We can separate the root *happy* from the prefix *un* and then say the word. Similarly, an unknown word such as *flying* can be figured out by separating the root *fly* from the inflectional ending *ing* (see Example 28 in Part II).

Structural analysis is not as utilitarian as phonics or context because not all unknown words contain structural units.

To summarize, it is obvious that analysis techniques are important. But how often should a reader have to use analysis techniques such as phonics or structural analysis when reading for either instructional or recreational purposes? If a child is given appropriate "just right" reading material, only a few words should be unknown. A good rule of thumb for narrative text is that at least 90–95% of the words on a page should be recognized at sight in order for a student to read the text without becoming frustrated and discouraged. In other words, no more than 5% or 10% of the words on the page would need to be sounded out. So, analysis techniques such as phonics are applicable only 5% or 10% of the time. They are "for emergency use only."

An Exception to the 90–95% Rule

When students read informational text, more than 10% of the words may be unknown to them. In such cases, they should not be expected to read the text unassisted. Instead, teachers should provide support in the form of vocabulary assistance, study guides, guided reading, and other aids.

Fluency

Fluency is the ability to orally and silently read text smoothly and with appropriate phrasing and intonation. We often refer to it as "reading like you talk." Fluency is not limited to oral reading. While oral reading is emphasized with emergent readers, the real fluency issue is how to help students become fluent *silent* readers.

Being fluent in both oral and silent reading is a function of:

1. How fast or slow one reads.
2. Whether the phrasing and intonation accurately reflects the meaning in the text.

Fluency is often determined by noting a reader's reading rate (words read per minute). However, the number of words read per minute does not take into account correct phrasing and intonation. To be an accurate measure of fluency, both speed and phrasing and intonation must be considered.

Fluency bridges comprehension and word identification. This is because fluency requires both recognizing most of the words on the page at sight (the word identification part) and proper phrasing and intonation reflective of the author's meaning (the comprehension part).

The comprehension part of fluency requires saying the words the way the author intended them to be said. It requires applying intonation and emphasis in ways consistent with the meaning in the text (see Example 29 in Part II).

The word identification part of fluency is the quick, smooth identification of words on the page. Stopping to correct miscues is a break in fluency. For this reason, fast, accurate recognition of easily confused words is an important fluency skill (see Example 30 in Part II).

Words per Minute

How fast should a reader be reading to be fluent? The usual standard is 90–120 words per minute. If a child is reading more slowly, there is probably a word recognition problem. That is, the student does not know all the words at sight. If a student is reading at more than 120 words per minute, it often sounds like speed reading in which phrasing and intonation are lost. The exception to these generalities, of course, is the emergent reader of any age who, naturally, reads more slowly at first.

Fluency is important because students seldom become enthusiastic readers until they experience what it means to be fluent. Reading just seems like too much hard work when you are not fluent.

How about English Language Learners?

English language learners (ELLs) often are in particular need of explicit explanations of comprehension and word identification. So what we teach ELL students is not different from what we teach English-speaking students. Like English speakers, ELLs must learn word meanings, comprehension strategies, word identification skills and strategies, and fluency strategies. The difference with ELLs is that we must put a very heavy emphasis on vocabulary (i.e., word meanings) and be more patient, more explicit, and more relentless in our explanations.

Summarizing Foundational Skills

Several misconceptions about foundational skills deserve emphasis. First, foundational skills are not taught first and comprehension later. Comprehension and foundational skills are both taught from the very beginning. Second, foundational skills are not just about phonics. To the contrary, what distinguishes fluent, motivated readers is their ability to recognize lots of words quickly. Phonics is an analysis technique and is slow, so it is difficult to be fluent if you depend solely on phonics to identify words.

Finally, the ultimate goal of foundational skills is to enable readers to use a combination of sight words, context, phonics, and (if there are structural units present) structural analysis to fluently comprehend text meaning.

SUMMARY

When children have rich language backgrounds at home, they learn comprehension and foundational skills easily. Struggling readers, however, often do not come to school with rich language backgrounds. For them, explicit explanations are often necessary. Part II of this book provides 30 examples of how to provide such explanations when teaching the Common Core standards. All are based on the principles of comprehension and foundational skills detailed in this chapter. When you adapt the Part II teaching examples to your particular situation, you must do so consistent with these principles.

Chapter 3

Emphasizing Large Ideas
as Well as the Nitty-Gritty

This book emphasizes the importance of explaining the nitty-gritty "how to" processes of reading standards, especially with struggling readers. But if that were all we did, students would construct only a narrow, technical concept of reading and writing. For students to understand reading in terms of language, literacy, and empowerment, we must also emphasize larger understandings. These larger understandings include:

- Reading and writing as communication.
- How the reading system works.
- Valuing reading.

These big understandings are often taken for granted. Typically, they do not get discussed during reading lessons, they do not get listed in reading programs or prescribed in commercial materials, and they are seldom tested as part of assessment systems. The Common Core itself, for instance, includes only a few of these big understandings.

Struggling readers, in particular, seldom understand how reading fits into a more global understanding of language, literacy, and communication. Instead, they often develop misconceptions about reading. For instance, because we necessarily emphasize decoding in kindergarten and first grade and spend lots of time on phonics, struggling readers often erroneously conclude that decoding is the main thing in reading when, in fact, we want them to understand that in the "big picture" comprehension is the important thing. Similarly, because accountability and high-stakes testing are such dominant parts of many classrooms today, struggling readers often erroneously conclude that passing the test is the important thing when, in fact, we want them to understand that in the "big picture" reading is important because it empowers you.

In many cases, we can eliminate those misconceptions by engaging students in literate tasks. But sometimes explicit talk is also necessary. For that reason, in each teaching example in Part II I have inserted a section called "Large Conceptual Ideas You Can Reinforce during This Lesson." It lists big ideas you might reinforce as you teach each particular lesson. It serves as a reminder that each reading lesson offers teachers opportunities to help students avoid narrow, technical learning by stating large conceptual ideas.

BIG UNDERSTANDINGS ABOUT READING AND WRITING AS COMMUNICATION

The heart of reading and writing is communication. We read to get an author's message; we write to communicate a message. Although it is important to engage students in tasks where they are actually reading text to get important messages and writing text to communicate important ideas, we also help students by making explicit statements about the message-sending and message-getting nature of reading and writing. For instance, we should always be looking for opportunities to make explicit statements about:

- Reading as a message-receiving system and writing as a message-sending system
- Students being authors when they write.
- Exchanges of notes being communicated.
- Reading as both enjoyment and as a practical tool.
- News reports in which reading made a real contribution or in which writing made a real contribution.
- The reciprocal nature of reading and writing.
- Reading as a problem-solving tool.

Assessing Students' Conceptual Understandings

How will you know students possess conceptual understandings? Like all informal assessment, the best way is to watch students during the normal course of the school day. For instance, when you observe things like the following, you can assume your students possess important big ideas.

- They talk about reading and writing as being messages.
- They talk about reading as useful in solving problems or accomplishing tasks.
- They talk about how various skills and strategies help them complete a task.
- They talk about literature as a source of understanding about living our lives.
- They talk about informational text in terms of how they will use what they have read or, alternatively, what they need to do next if a text did not provide the information needed for the task at hand.

BIG UNDERSTANDINGS
ABOUT HOW THE READING SYSTEM WORKS

Reading and writing are not random processes; they are parts of a system. We use an agreed upon set of conventions to interpret and make sense of written text and to construct our written messages. When students have understandings about how skills, strategies, and standards fit into the larger language system, the quality of their learning improves. Consequently, it is helpful to look for opportunities to make explicit statements such as the following:

- Reading and writing use a top-to-bottom and right-to-left system.
- The reading and writing systems are based on an alphabet code.
- White spaces between words tell us where one word ends and another begins.
- Good readers recognize most words at sight and use phonics as an "emergency only" technique.
- Reading and writing are reciprocal processes; what is learned in reading can be applied to writing, and what is learned in writing can be applied to reading.
- You cannot be passive when comprehending; comprehension requires proactive and assertive construction of meaning based on careful analysis of text cues and one's prior knowledge.

- Authors and readers may be operating from different sets of experiences, so the meaning a reader constructs may not be precisely the same meaning an author intended.
- All comprehension requires inferring; all predictions are "best guesses" based on text cues and the reader's prior knowledge.
- Comprehending always includes predicting–monitoring–repredicting in a continuous cycle.
- Expert reading begins before you start reading and continues after you have turned the last page.
- There are no rules in comprehension—it requires tentative predictions and proactive thought adjusted to the situation.
- There are different kinds of text for different kinds of purposes.
- Authors organize text in ways that best communicate their message; readers comprehend better if they recognize the organization the author is employing.
- "Close reading" for deep understanding is essential and cannot be accomplished casually.

Some of these examples are included as standards in the Common Core, but most are not. Consequently, it is important to look for opportunities to be explicit about these big understandings.

Examples of Explaining the Reading System

Kindergarten and first-grade teachers often read aloud large experience charts or "big books," and, as they do so, they run their fingers under the print from left to right while saying, "good readers start at the left and go across the print like this." Similarly, early primary-grade teachers sometimes allow note passing in their classrooms, and they use this activity to make explicit statements about the message-sending and message-getting nature of language. Upper-grade teachers make explicit statements about the different text structures encountered in informational text. And teachers at all grade levels emphasize verbally (and then reemphasize, again and again) that good readers are assertive in building meaning and do not wait passively for meaning to come to them. All these big understandings help students see how the reading system works.

BIG UNDERSTANDINGS ABOUT VALUING READING

A prevalent instructional problem is the tendency of students to learn skills, strategies, and standards without understanding why they are learning them. They learn for the test; or they learn because they are told to, or they learn to get a grade on a report card. But they do not see how the learning of skills, strategies, and standards has anything to do with becoming enriched, or enabled, or empowered, or literate. In short, they do not see a value in reading and writing, so they just go through the motions.

From an instructional perspective, this problem is often discussed as a problem of teaching skills, strategies, and standards in isolation from real reading. From students' perspective, it is often discussed as a lack of student "agency," or lack of student "ownership" of the content, or lack of motivation.

Regardless of how it is labeled, there is a big, important idea here: Reading and writing instruction fails unless students end up valuing reading and writing.

One reason students fail to value reading may lie with our prevailing view that the key to motivation is students' interest in what they read. We ask, "Did students enjoy the activity?" but we do not ask, "Did students value what they read?" As a consequence, we end up knowing more about students' affect for a reading activity and do not know whether students see what they are reading as having value to them or having potential for improving their lives.

The Common Core recognizes the need for students to value reading. To ensure that they do, a featured standard is "reading for purpose and understanding." Similarly, this book recognizes this problem and embeds every teaching example "inside" an authentic task in which students are "reading for purpose and understanding." In both cases, the goal is for students to value what they read because it results in a valued outcome, rather than because it happens to be interesting.

By providing such authentic tasks, many students learn on their own to value reading. But some also need explicit statements about the value of reading. That is, teachers need to talk not only about what is to be learned and how to do it, but also about why it is being learned and when it will be used. Psychologists refer to this as "conditional knowledge"— knowledge about why and when. By making explicit conditional knowledge statements during instruction, teachers help students learn to value reading. Examples of such explicit statements include the following.

- Specifying in each lesson's objective how the particular skill, strategy, or standard will be immediately applied in a real reading situation.

- Stating for each lesson what action students will be able to take or what problem will be solved as a result of being able to apply the skill, strategy, or standard being emphasized.

- Deemphasizing the interest value of a particular text and emphasizing its value in enabling students to do something they desire to do.

- Citing examples of how specific reading and writing activities have empowered, enabled, and/or enriched us.

Establishing this "big understanding" is challenging. School is an inherently artificial place. What seems to count most are test scores, workbooks, and report cards. In this environment, it is often unclear whether students ever realize that skills, strategies, and standards can transform their lives. It is crucial, therefore, that we do whatever we can to communicate this big understanding to students.

Examples of Explaining the Value of Reading

Teachers committed to developing students who value reading ensure that students are reading for purpose and understanding and routinely locate skills, strategies, and standards instruction "inside" authentic literacy tasks. But, additionally, they make explicit statements about the value of reading. For instance:

- Teachers have public celebrations when problems are solved by reference to text;

- When students accomplish a goal by reading, teachers point out how the skill, strategy, or standard was a stepping stone to what really counted.

- When preparing students for achievement tests, teachers keep reminding students that the tests are important for the school district but that for them personally the tests are not as important as being able to solve problems through reading and writing.

- When introducing lessons, teachers routinely point out that what they are learning will help students accomplish "real" reading and writing tasks.

- Teachers reserve their highest student praise for occasions when students are empowered, enabled, or ennobled through the use of reading and writing.

How Will You Know Students Value Reading?

You will know students value reading if you observe behaviors such as the following:

- They laugh out loud when reading a novel.
- They insist on sneaking in a page or two of reading when you want them to be doing something else.
- When problems arise, they suggest things to read to solve the problem.
- They spontaneously turn to the Internet to find the answers to questions.

SUMMARY

To us as teachers, many of the foregoing large understandings seem obvious. We sometimes think they are so obvious that no explicit talk is needed. We take them for granted, and we seldom talk about them. Strict adherence to the Common Core standards, for instance, would result in ignoring some very important global understandings about reading as language and as literacy.

This can be a serious omission, especially for students who do not "catch on" easily. They often develop misconceptions about reading and writing, and those misconceptions frequently turn reading into a technical activity having no compelling purpose, or overall structure, or value. It is important, therefore, to talk directly about these big understandings. The suggestions provided for each Part II teaching example will be helpful in keeping these "big understandings" at the forefront of students' minds.

Chapter 4

How to Use Part II
of This Book

Part II is the heart of this book. It provides 30 examples of how to explain the standards specified by the Common Core State Standards for English Language Arts. This chapter prepares you to use these examples.

The examples are provided in the expectation that they will be used only when you determine that your students, or a small group of your students, cannot meet a particular standard. When that time comes, Part II is organized to help you find the teaching example you need. The teaching examples match the order of the Common Core standards, providing first samples for explaining each type of Literature standard, then each type of Informational Text standard, and finally each type of Foundational Skills standard. I ordered the teaching examples in this way so that when you need to teach to a particular Common Core standard, you can locate it in this book in the same place you find the standard listed in the Common Core.

At the start of each Part II teaching example, the specific standard being illustrated is identified in parentheses after the example number and topic. For instance, Example 1 connects to the first Literature standard, which is one of three standards that address Key Ideas and Details. Therefore, you will see "Key Ideas and Details—RL Standard 1" in parentheses under the title.

While the Common Core includes 10 reading standards for Literature, 10 for Informational Text, and 4 for Foundational Skills, Part II has 30 teaching examples because the Common Core occasionally includes more than one kind of skill or strategy in a single standard. For instance, the first standard for Literature includes both "reading for details" and "inference." In teaching to this standard, however, we must first teach students how to read for details and then teach them how to infer. Consequently, Part II includes two sample lessons for Standard 1 in Literature: one on Reading for Key Details (Example 1) and one on Drawing Inferences (Example 2).

It is also true that the Common Core sometimes repeats the same standard for both literature and informational text. For instance, reading for details is a standard for literature and is also a standard for informational text. When that duplication occurs, I have inserted a note indicating that the example provided for literature can also be used when teaching the same thing in informational text.

In creating each Part II teaching example, I arbitrarily selected one grade level to illustrate how to teach that type of standard. For instance, Example 1 focuses on "Reading for Key Details," and I used the seventh-grade standard as my example (*RL.7.1: Cite several pieces of textual evidence to support analysis of what the text says*). The basic explanation I provide for each example is as generic as I can make it in order for you to adapt it for use at other grade levels. While the level of sophistication and text difficulty changes substantially from grade to grade, the basic elements of the verbal explanation do not change as much from grade to grade.

HOW THE PART II TEACHING EXAMPLES ARE ORGANIZED

Each teaching example in Part II is presented in five parts: Background, Pre-Lesson Consideration, Organizing for Instruction, The Lesson, and Post-Lesson Considerations.

Background

The background section describes the Common Core standard on which the example is based, provides general assistance regarding the teaching of that standard, notes prerequisites that must be in place before teaching that standard, and suggests how the example could be adapted to other grade levels.

Is Explanation Just for Struggling Readers?

Explicit explanations are used mostly with struggling readers. But occasionally good readers also need explanations. It is not uncommon, for instance, to find good readers who struggle when faced with doing what the Common Core calls "close reading." In these cases, you may want to use Part II examples even though the student is not a struggling reader.

Pre-Lesson Considerations

There are two pre-lesson considerations. First, explanations should always be rooted in assessment. Consequently, each Part II teaching example is meant to be used after you have done "kid watching" and have reason to believe certain students are not ready to meet that standard. The pre-instruction assessment suggestions in Part II describe what to look for when using "kid watching" to assess whether students are ready to meet a particular standard.

Second, as specified in Chapter 3, reading is learned best when it is rooted in big understandings about why we read and write, how the reading and writing systems work, and the valuing of reading and writing. Anything you can do to keep these large ideas in students' minds will improve their learning. Each Part II teaching example provides reminders of some of the particularly important big understandings relevant to that lesson.

Organizing for Instruction

For illustrative purposes, each example in Part II is grounded in a hypothetical reading task. This task involves an authentic purpose for reading a particular text or set of texts. The goal is to help students learn to value reading as empowering, enabling, and ennobling. As noted in Chapter 1 (and as specified in the Common Core standard labeled "Range of Reading and Level of Text Complexity"), standards should be taught in conjunction with real reading activity using real text in which the goal is reading for purpose and understanding. Consistent with the knowledge-building emphasis of the Common Core, the tasks I suggest in many Part II examples are based on content areas such as social studies and science.

Because this book is a resource rather than a script, the authentic reading task I describe will give you an idea about what you could do, but you will use different texts and different tasks. In creating your own "reading for purpose and understanding" tasks, the guiding principle is that students should feel there is a compelling reason to complete the task.

There are times when it makes sense to teach a particular standard to the whole class, and I include some examples of those among the 30 teaching examples. Most of the time, however, the reality of individual student differences cannot be ignored and pre-instruction assessment reveals that some students will be ready to meet the standard being assessed and some students will not. As a result, you must organize instruction to include differentiation, with you providing direct instruction on the standard to a small group of students or to an individual student while other students are doing something else. This section suggests what you might have those other students doing. There are many ways to differentiate instruction, and how you decide to do it will be your choice. The purpose of this section is to provide a variety of different ideas from which you may choose.

Overcoming Students' Fear of Failure

When students struggle with one or another aspect of reading, it is difficult to combat their defensiveness and reluctance to try. Typically, struggling readers have experienced past failure. Like all humans, they try to avoid continued failure. Consequently, you often hear them say something like "I can't do this" or "I don't want to do this." Invariably, their reactions are rooted in fear of embarrassment if they do not succeed. Overcoming student reluctance to respond requires teacher artfulness and sensitivity. As teachers, our instinctive response is to reassure students by telling them the task is easy. But, in actuality, we should say, "This is a hard task. Not everybody gets it right the first time." Doing so protects students' egos. If they fail to get it the first time, it is okay because it was hard, and not everybody gets it the first time. They are like lots of other people, and that's okay. When we tell them it is easy, however, students are not protected when they struggle. We told them it was easy, but for them it was hard. They feel dumb, and they become even more reluctant to respond.

The Lesson

The lesson consists of six parts: the objective, introducing the lesson, stating the secret to doing it, modeling the thinking, scaffolded assistance, and continued application to reading.

Stating the Objective

Explanation is intentional teaching. We intentionally set out to prepare students to meet a specific Common Core standard. To be effective, we need to be clear about what we are trying to accomplish. The best way to ensure clarity is to make the objective public. In addition, when students know what they are trying to learn, they are better able to learn it.

Consequently, we tell students what they will learn and why it is important. Each example in Part II includes an illustrative objective.

Objectives are stated in observable terms so that we (and our students) can tell whether the objective was achieved and that learning has occurred. Consequently, the sample examples start with:

"By the end of this lesson, you will be able to. . . ."

and goes on to state exactly what students will be able to do, as in the example below:

"By the end of this lesson you will be able to make predictions before you read by using the title of the story as your clue, and you will be able to tell us how you made the prediction."

Why Make Objectives Public?

Making objectives known to students helps them learn. If the objectives are vague or unstated, students are left to guess what they should be trying to do; if the objective is stated publicly, students know what to focus on. In some schools, teachers begin every lesson by putting the objective on a 5″ × 8″ note card or on a piece of paper, and posting it for students to read at the beginning of the lesson. Students and teacher then reexamine the objective at the end of the lesson to check to see if the objective was met. Making objectives public and explicit helps "demystify" the process of learning to read by clarifying what students are accountable for in a particular lesson.

Introducing the Lesson

All students (but especially struggling readers) learn best when they know what the purpose is or what they are supposed to accomplish. So each teaching example in Part II includes a sample introductory statement you can use to guide you in introducing your own explanations. Each includes statements of:

- A reference to the task being pursued (the "reading for purpose and understanding" specified above).
- A statement of what students will be learning.
- How it will be used (i.e., why they are learning it).

For example:

> "We are reading this story today to collect information we can use in our project on whales. But we are also going to learn to use clues from the title to make predictions about what is going to happen in the story we read today. For each prediction, you will be able to tell me how you used the title as a clue to come up with your predictions. We will then use what we learned about making predictions as we continue on our project about whales."

Note that the introduction specifies not only the objective (what will be learned) but also *why* it will be learned (i.e., when it will be used). This is a link to the "reading for purpose and understanding" noted above and to the Chapter 3 emphasis on building big understandings about valuing reading. Including such a statement is a form of motivation because when students know that what they are learning is to be immediately put to work in an authentic task, they are more likely to put forth the necessary effort and are more likely to value reading.

Stating the "Secret" to Doing It

There is a "secret" (or "secrets") to doing any task successfully. For instance:

A golf instructor teaches neophyte golfers the "secrets" to striking the ball correctly.

A flight instructor teaches neophyte pilots the "secrets" to navigating an airplane under instrument conditions.

Reading, too, has its "secrets." But the secrets of reading are more subtle than the secrets for playing golf or flying an airplane, because reading is a cognitive task heavily influenced by differences in background knowledge. Because of these differences, different people think differently about how to do a skill or strategy, particularly in comprehension. Consequently, although each Part II teaching example provides a "secret" to doing a particular skill or strategy, be cautioned that the "secret" is a representative example, not a universal procedure. Not every student will use what the teacher states in exactly the same way the teacher uses it.

Good readers often figure out the secrets for themselves. But this seldom happens with struggling readers. Reading tasks often remain a mystery to them. Directing them to the secret minimizes that problem. When they are given explicit information, they are better able to adjust what we say to their own way of thinking and to put it to work in the reading of real text.

As teachers, we are expert readers; we read without conscious thought or effort. So we are sometimes at a loss to tell students what the secret is. The Part II examples are designed to be a resource when this happens.

Students as Explainers

Explicit explanations are sometimes erroneously associated solely with teachers. However, teachers are not the only ones who can explain how to meet Common Core standards. Often, students bring to the classroom valuable experiences and understandings about how to do things. It is almost always beneficial for students who possess such understandings to share them with other students.

Modeling the Thinking

Modeling how to read is not like demonstrating a physical task such as tying your shoes. We cannot physically demonstrate how reading works because reading is thinking. It occurs in the mind and is invisible.

The only way to model thinking is to talk about how to do it. That is, we provide a verbal description of the thinking one does or, more accurately, an *approximation* of the thinking involved (since there is no one way to do most reading skills or strategies). The information we provide gives students a "toehold" on how to do the thinking, and they gradually make it their own during the scaffolding that follows.

Modeling versus Questioning

It is hard for us to resist questioning students while teaching. Our instinct is to use questions as a device to keep their attention. But if you have correctly assessed the situation, you know students are unable to meet the standard being addressed. So it is counterproductive to start a lesson by asking them to meet the standard. Instead, questioning should be reserved for scaffolding. Prior to that, you provide the needed information about what to pay attention to (the secret) and how to do it (modeling the thinking). While this amount of uninterrupted teacher talk will be new to many students, they will respond to it well if you explain why you are doing such talking and make clear that they will be much more fully involved later in the scaffolding. It may take some time, but students soon adjust.

Modeling Does Not Mean Rule Following

Learning to do a skill or strategy is, to some degree, an individual process. No two people process information in precisely the same way. Therefore, modeling how to do a skill or strategy does not mean giving students rules to follow. Your explanation is, instead, your attempt to provide a *representative* example of the thinking one does. It should be made clear that students are to use your modeling as a guide, not as a script to follow.

When we model, we provide a verbal statement of how to perform a skill or strategy or standard. We talk about the thinking we do in as clear and explicit a way as possible. Consequently, modeling is often described as "think-alouds" or as "mental modeling." We talk out loud about how *we* do the invisible thinking involved so that our students can use our model as a starting point for developing *their* way of doing it.

An Example of a "Think-Aloud"

"Let me show you how to make predictions. Pay attention to what I do so you can use it as a starting point when you try to do predictions. When I make predictions, I look at the topic we are reading about and I think about what I already know about that topic and base my prediction on that experience. I say to myself, 'What does my experience tell me is likely to be happening in this story?' For instance, this story has the word *circus* in the title, so I think to myself, 'What do I already know about circuses?' Then I say, 'I have been to a circus. What happened when I went to the circus is probably what will happen in this story.' And so my prediction is based on what I already know from my experience."

How Explicit Must the Modeling Be?

The key to good modeling is providing enough information to "demystify" the process for students. When modeling how to make an inference, for instance, it is not enough to say, "I am thinking that they are afraid someone is going to see them." The modeling is more likely to be helpful if it includes why you think what you think: "Using my background knowledge and the clue in the text about trying to blend into the surroundings, I think to myself that if that were me it would mean I don't want to be noticed. So using what I know from my own experience about the clue in the text, I infer that this person in the story is staying with the crowd so he won't be noticed."

Each example in Part II of this book illustrates how one might mental model or "think-aloud" about the standard in question. Each of those examples is tied to a particular piece of text and to a particular task, so you will need to adapt them to the text and the task you are using. However, the intent of each example is to give you enough information for you to construct your own "think-aloud."

Scaffolded Assistance

Scaffolding is a process of helping students move from our modeling of the thinking to their independent application of the standard. Scaffolds are temporary supports, with much support provided initially and then gradually reduced as the student gains confidence in responding. We give students opportunities to try out what we modeled, with lots of help from us at first, and then gradually with less and less help.

Because modeling usually provides students only with a toehold, they need scaffolds, or crutches, when they first try to do what we modeled. The goal is to move from teacher ownership to student ownership. At first, students are dependent on our assistance. But as we gradually reduce the amount of assistance, students gain experience in responding and build their own understandings. That is, they personalize the task and make it their own. They assume metacognitive control.

What Is "Metacognitive Control"?

Cognitive psychologists define *metacognition* as "thinking about one's thinking." It can also be described as "becoming conscious of your mental processes when reading." Metacognition is important in reading because students become better readers if they are conscious of what they are doing. We don't want them to become what a colleague of mine calls "strategy spitters"—students who simply mimic the teacher's talk. So a major purpose of explicit explanations is for students to become conscious of what they are doing when reading. When we say we want to put students in metacognitive control, we are saying we don't want them to be "strategy spitters." We want them to be conscious of what they are doing and why. To ensure that this happens, it is important to ask students to describe the thinking they did, and for you to use your judgment to determine whether what a student says is genuine understanding or just mimicry.

There are five keys to scaffolded assistance:

1. Using cues and crutches to focus students on key elements (that is, on the "secret").
2. Gradually reducing the amount of assistance only when students show evidence of achieving the objective (with you being prepared to differentiate instruction further for those students who require more time).
3. Observing each student's responses closely to determine whether the student is keeping initial predictions in mind, making sense of the cues provided, and making reasoned (rather than shallow or casual) responses.
4. Changing or modifying a cue or crutch on-the-fly in response to students' restructured understandings.
5. Noting whether students are actually using the skill or strategy when pursuing real reading tasks.

Examples of Scaffolded Assistance

We used to teach swimming with "water wings"—balloon-like wings inflated with air and placed under the child's armpits. They kept the child afloat as he or she tried to swim. As he or she became more competent as a swimmer, the air in the wings was gradually reduced until the child was swimming without the assistance of the wings. The wings served as a temporary support, or scaffold. Similarly, young baseball players learn to hit the ball off a tee before facing a pitcher. The tee is a crutch, or temporary scaffold. In reading, scaffolded assistance may take the form of visual cues, or auditory emphasis, or leading questions by the teacher, depending on the nature of the task. These are crutches, or scaffolds, to help students gradually get to the point of doing the task independently.

The length of time spent on scaffolded assistance depends entirely on how quickly students learn. Sometimes a student catches on after just a few responses, and sometimes assistance must be provided over several days or weeks. The key is to watch students' responses. If they respond satisfactorily, assistance can be reduced and ultimately eliminated. If they respond in ways that reveal confusion or hesitation, you may need to continue providing help and sometimes increase the amount of help. It requires patience and close observation of students. You can't hurry students' learning of standards. For struggling readers particularly, it takes time.

Each teaching example in Part II of this book provides three levels of scaffolding to illustrate that assistance is gradually reduced. However, the examples in Part II are only suggestive. You will often need more than three levels of scaffolding, and your success will depend on how skillfully you modify the scaffolds you invented to fit students' emerging understandings during the lesson. Teacher thought is essential because students respond differently. Consequently, you need to be ready to make spontaneous decisions about how to adjust the scaffolding if students demonstrate hesitancy, misconceptions, or misunderstanding.

Artfulness Is Required during Scaffolding

Students are always constructing understandings. They do so on the basis of their past experiences. Often these experiences are not congruent with what we say in our explanations. In those cases, students may restructure the information we provide and develop erroneous or misleading understandings. To minimize this problem, pay close attention to students' responses during scaffolded assistance, using student responses as "windows into their minds" to determine what sense they are making of the lesson. Often student responses during scaffolded assistance reveal a misconception or confusion. When that happens, adjust on-the-fly by altering the scaffolded assistance in ways that get students to construct a more accurate understanding.

Continued Application to Reading

During the lesson introduction, we state why we are learning the skill or strategy or standard and when it would be used. It is in the "Continued Application" section of the lesson that it *is* used—in the "reading for purpose and understanding" task specified at the beginning of the lesson. Application is an integral part of explanation because we cannot say instruction has been successful until we see students transfer it to real reading. Hence, all the Part II examples include application. Students should know from the beginning of the lesson that application in real reading is the goal.

The Part II examples include three different models of application. Some examples model how you can explain a standard and then have students apply it later when reading text; some demonstrate how you can teach a standard at the same time a text is being read; and some demonstrate how you can teach a standard after reading a selection. These models are provided for illustrative purposes. You will decide for yourself the kind of application to use in any particular lesson.

Post-Lesson Considerations

Two considerations are important after the lesson. First, you need to know if a lesson has been successful—that is, whether students are applying what they learned in the reading of real text and are now ready to meet that particular Common Core standard. As with the pre-instruction assessment, you can assess a lesson's success by "kid watching."

Post-instruction assessment is essential. Because we taught it does not mean they learned it. In fact, in the real world of classrooms, struggling readers seldom master an objective completely the first time. We need to know how well a student is doing at the end of a lesson in order to decide where to go from here. Is immediate re-teaching necessary? Or can we can move on to other standards and return to this one later? Post-instruction assessment is key in making these decisions.

Second, whenever possible, reading instruction and writing instruction should be linked. Because reading and writing are reciprocal activities, most reading standards are reflected in writing. Consequently, it is often effective to teach a reciprocal writing skill or strategy in conjunction with the teaching of a reading standard. Each example in Part II, therefore, includes suggestions for how to link the reading lesson to a Common Core writing standard.

SUMMARY

This book emphasizes the view that direct and explicit teacher explanation is an important alternative tool when students do not learn easily and are struggling to meet Common Core standards. The 30 teaching examples provided in Part II will be useful resources when explanation becomes necessary. But, as noted in the next chapter, the teaching examples will be helpful only if you implement them in professional and adaptive ways.

Chapter 5

Professional Judgment and Teaching to Standards

This book emphasizes explicit explanation. The research on explicit explanations is clear: Explaining explicitly is effective, particularly with struggling readers.

But another, even more important finding, also resulted from the research. While all the teachers were explicit, not all were effective. The *least effective* teachers faithfully followed my suggestions for how to be explicit; the *most effective* teachers often changed my suggestions for how to be explicit.

So why were those who faithfully followed my directions less effective? It happened because reading instruction is a complex endeavor, and it is impossible for me or for any one else to predict in advance exactly what to do or say. The most effective teachers recognized this, took charge of their instruction, and adapted my instructional suggestions to fit their particular situation.

This book is driven by both findings. Yes, explicit explanations are effective, and the Part II teaching examples are based on that finding. But, additionally, because we know effective teachers use their professional judgment rather than following suggestions faithfully, I assume you will do likewise.

This chapter describes how. It suggests four ways in which effective teachers exercise professional judgment when implementing explicit explanations of standards: they balance seemingly contradictory aspects of explicit instruction, they engage in nitty-gritty kinds of decision making at each stage of explanation, they bring to the teaching task a mental strength based on a clear understanding of themselves and why they teach reading, and they are realistic about the nature of their work.

48

BALANCING ACTS

Effective teachers understand that explicit explanations do not occur in isolation and that standards are a relatively small part of a larger instructional endeavor. Getting this concept across to students requires you to engage in some mental balancing acts.

First, in an environment in which standards seem to be the most important thing, you must engage students in high-challenge literacy tasks. As noted in Chapter 1, engaging students in genuinely literate activity is a fundamental principle. Achieving this end is a delicate balancing act because you must do two seemingly contradictory things simultaneously. On the one hand, you must ensure that your students understand the importance of standards and of what you do to ensure that they meet standards. On the other hand, *your students must understand that explicit explanations of standards are relatively minor parts of their classroom lives, and that what really counts is pursuit of authentic literacy tasks.* Balancing these requires thoughtful decisions and professional judgment.

Second, and closely related to the first point, you must ensure that your reading program itself is balanced. That means that the Common Core standards do not dominate, that explicit explanations are used selectively on an "as-needed" basis, and that many other forms of reading and writing prevail. What constitutes "balance" in your classroom is a judgment call. It differs from teacher to teacher. The other kinds of literate activity you choose to employ and how much time you spend on each is your decision. You are the one who knows best what your students need, what the local situation demands, and what constraints may be imposed by administrators. So you must decide what "balance" is going to look like in your classroom. But whatever you decide, *you want to ensure that meeting Common Core standards is important while simultaneously ensuring that it will not be the dominant literacy activity in the classroom.* It is another balancing act requiring careful teacher thought.

Finally, you must put students in the "driver's seat" when, in fact, the very nature of explicit explanations seems to put you in the "driver's seat." It is the teacher who does most of the initial talking and who remains in control throughout the scaffolding process. This initial control is necessary because struggling readers seldom have enough background experience to figure things out for themselves. But while teacher control is essential at first, *it is equally essential that you make the priority goal that of putting students in control of their own efforts to make sense out of text.* While being in control yourself as the lesson begins, you must make clear that students will soon be expected to take charge themselves. Accomplishing these seemingly contradictory requirements is another balancing act requiring professional judgment and thoughtful decision making.

LESSON DECISIONS

The most effective teachers do not rigidly follow the teaching examples I provide in Part II. Rather, they make numerous decisions at virtually every stage of explanation. Ten of these decisions are described next.

Decisions about Who Gets Explanations When

Explanation is a selective technique. You explain only for students who need it. It would be wrong to force a student to endure an explanation if he or she can already meet the standard.

Consequently, a diagnostic approach is required. Like a doctor who determines whether you are sick before prescribing medication, you determine whether students need explanations before providing them.

The Part II suggestions for pre- and post-instruction assessment will assist you in doing such diagnoses. If the data you collect indicate students can already meet a particular standard, do not explain; if the data suggest they are *not* ready, do explain. But be prepared to make two kinds of decisions. First, the assessments I provide are all informal techniques, so you will need to use professional judgment in deciding who does and who does not need explicit instruction. Second, once you decide who needs instruction and who does not, you will need to figure out how to organize your classroom so that you can teach those who need it while those who do not need it are doing something else.

Decisions about Keeping Students Motivated

Explicit explanation is typically employed with struggling readers who are difficult to motivate. Two kinds of decisions are important in keeping struggling readers motivated.

Struggling readers struggle because, for them, reading is difficult. They resist reading because they look like failures when they read. And as I've said previously, like all humans, they avoid what makes them feel like failures. So if you want motivated readers, first stop insisting that they read difficult material (unless you are right there to provide instructional support). Instead, have them read easy material and, when they succeed, praise them lavishly. They may temporarily complain that it is "baby stuff," but ultimately the feeling of success will prevail over the former feeling of failure. And with success, students become more willing to take a risk, and you can gradually introduce them to more and more difficult levels of instruction.

Second, to keep students motivated you have to engage them in tasks they think are sensible and worth their effort. The "reading for purpose and understanding" tasks illustrated in all the Part II examples are designed to be sensible, to be worth students' efforts, and likely to help students learn to value reading. But those examples cannot be used as presented in Part II. You must develop your own. Doing so is difficult because "real-life" tasks seldom occur naturally in school and must, therefore, be created. But despite the difficulty, if your goal is to promote student motivation, every lesson requires engaging students in tasks they see as worth their effort. To accomplish this difficult task, some teachers establish long-running projects, form semipermanent groupings such as book clubs or literature circles, or establish classroom newspapers. Whatever you decide on, "reading for purpose and understanding" must be a compelling task that also offers the possibility of teaching to a Common Core standard "inside" that larger task.

Decisions about What Text to Use

One of the essential messages of this book is that the Common Core standards should be explained using real text (i.e., students should be "reading for purpose and understanding"). This is often a vexing problem because appropriate text is difficult to locate. To teach to a particular standard, you need a text that offers opportunities to use that standard while also fitting the purpose for reading.

Searching for such text is time-consuming. There is always the dream that someone will provide us with a list of suitable texts or that a commercial program will provide all we need. But no one but you can ensure the vitality and motivation that come from engaging students in texts they see as important to read at that moment.

So, while text selection is often time-consuming and sometimes requires settling for less-than-ideal examples, it is nevertheless an essential decision in effective explanation of the Common Core standards. The text examples provided in Part II can serve as a model, but you will need to decide on the actual texts yourself.

Decisions about Applying a Part II Example to Other Grade Levels

The Common Core standards are organized in levels, moving from less complex versions of a standard at kindergarten and first grade to more complex versions of the standard at seventh and eighth grade. In order to illustrate how to explain a particular standard, I arbitrarily picked a grade level to illustrate how that particular type of standard could be explained. Each example provides a generic explanation that can be adapted to other grade levels with little change.

In the introduction to each example, I have tried to provide assistance regarding how the explanation I provide can be adapted to other grade levels. Nevertheless, your situation will be different: Your students will be different, the text you will be using will be different, and the "reading for purpose and understanding" will be different. While the generic explanation I provide for any standard includes the essential elements for meeting that standard, you will nevertheless need to use your professional judgment to make decisions about how my example can be adapted to your situation.

Decisions about Stating the Student's Objective

While the Part II teaching examples provide a sample objective for each Common Core standard, you will need to decide for yourself how you will tie the objective to the text to be used. Also, while it is always good practice to make the objective public, how you ultimately decide to do that will be your decision.

Decisions about Stating the Secret to Doing It

The examples in Part II are my best efforts to provide generic statements of what the "secret" is for successfully meeting various Common Core standards. I am confident they will be helpful much of the time. However, because students come from different backgrounds, and/or have different learning styles, and/or have idiosyncratic misconceptions, my suggestions may not always suffice.

Consequently, you must be prepared for students who, when you describe the secret, give you puzzled looks. It will happen. And when it does, you will need to make an on-the-fly decision about how to modify the secret in response to the student.

Decisions about Modeling the Thinking

The modeling examples I provide in Part II are tied to a hypothetical group of students and to a hypothetical task I create to illustrate "reading for purpose and understanding." You will have different students and different "real reading" tasks. Consequently, you will have to make a decision about how to fit the modeling to your situation and to your students.

Also, you will often need to adjust your modeling by shortening it or, alternatively, by adding more detail. For instance, some students may not need as extensive an explanation as I suggest while others will need more detailed modeling or repeated modeling. You will have to be the judge, and you will have to make the necessary decisions.

Decisions about Scaffolded Assistance

As emphasized in Chapter 4, scaffolded assistance requires much teacher thought and artfulness. In my own teaching, I find that no matter how carefully I plan the scaffolding, students' responses during instruction cause me to make on-the-fly decisions. Sometimes students catch on quickly, and I can abandon some of the planned scaffolding; more often, they restructure my explanation in ways I had not anticipated, requiring me to create more extensive scaffolds and/or crutches. Such spontaneous decision making is essential if explanations are to be effective.

Consequently, the three levels of scaffolded assistance I suggest are illustrative only. They will give you a start, but you will need to make proactive decisions of your own to ensure that your students receive the help they need to "own" the skill, strategy, or standard.

Decisions about Application to Reading

As I have emphasized throughout, explanations isolated from application in real reading are seldom helpful to students. While I provide application suggestions, you will need to decide how to adapt my suggestions to your particular situation.

One of the most difficult aspects of application is finding the time for it. In my imaginary examples in Part II, lessons are not constrained by time limitations. But in real classrooms, time is always an issue. So you will often need to parcel out lessons over several days, especially when working with struggling readers. In that time crunch, it is crucial to find time for application, despite the difficulty involved in making that decision.

Decisions about Links to the Common Core Writing Standards

Each example in Part II includes a suggestion about how it could be linked to a Common Core writing standard. Integrating reading and writing instruction is a frequently overlooked but powerful technique for strengthening both reading and writing. From the very beginning stages of learning to read and write, we should make sure students know that what we are learning in reading can be applied in writing and vice versa.

What I provide is suggestive. It is usually limited to pointing out which Common Core writing standard is reciprocal to (or closely related to) the reading standard being illustrated. You must exercise your own judgment in deciding how you will link particular Common Core reading standards to matching Common Core writing standards.

MENTAL STRENGTH

An important professional aspect of teaching is a teacher's strong personal commitment. Excellent teachers are sometimes called "caring teachers;" sometimes they are called "passionate teachers;" and sometimes they are called teachers "teaching with their hair on fire." All refer to the fact that the best teachers have a high level of commitment.

Commitment requires mental strength. The source of that strength is based in your analysis of why you are teaching and what you are committed to (i.e., the impact you want to have on students). This analysis results in a vision for how you want your students to use reading in their lives, or what it is you want them to value about reading.

Vision makes "reading for purpose and understanding" more than a slogan. The vision defines what kind of reading should be dominant and what kind of tasks students should pursue when "reading for purpose and understanding." For some teachers, the driving vision is that students will be empowered and, in those situations, "reading for purpose and understanding" involves engaging students in reading tasks that help them see they are having a tangible impact, as when they read to make the playground safer or to convince lawmakers to save the whales. For other teachers, the driving vision might be social justice, and, in those cases, "reading for purpose and understanding" involves engaging students in reading tasks about how to improve services to the homeless or how to help the elderly. Still other teachers envision reading as a practical tool, and, in those cases, "reading for purpose and understanding" involves engaging students in reading of application forms, driver's tests, newspapers, recipes, and reference materials. Teachers who have a vision know the impact they want to have, and they orchestrate classroom tasks to give students experience with what reading can do for them.

It is not important what vision a teacher has. What is important is that the teacher *has* a vision. That is, what is important is that you analyze what you are committed to accomplishing and what impact you want to have in the world through your students. It is similar to the old statement, "I touch the future; I teach" but it can be restated as "I have a vision for my students, so I know how I will touch the future."

Developing a vision requires hard thinking and professional judgment, but it results in confidence and strength that will sustain your commitment when things get tough. In a world of high-stakes testing, for instance, in which the pressure to meet standards can become intrusive, teachers who have a clear vision are able, despite the pressure, to remain passionate about their work, to be relentless in helping struggling readers, and to find ways to creatively involve students in "reading for purpose and understanding."

In summary, vision takes teaching out of the realm of being "a job" and moves it into the realm of being a service to the future.

REALISTIC EXPECTATIONS

Of all the things that distinguish effective from less effective teachers, perhaps the most important is the expectations they set for themselves. These expectations take two forms.

The first and most commonly discussed aspect of expectation is the principle that people tend to achieve to the level they set for themselves. So, given that principle, to become a high achiever you should set high expectations for yourself. This is certainly true in teaching. The most effective teachers are the ones who set goals that are seemingly out of reach, who refuse to give up on students, and who are relentless in their attempts to improve themselves and their teaching.

However, a less frequently discussed, but perhaps more important, aspect of the expectancy principle is that of being realistic. That is, while it is important to set high expectations for your teaching, it is equally important to be able to accept not always meeting those expectations. This is particularly important because teaching is an impossible task. Everyone around you seems to expect you to be successful with all students all the time. But we know that's impossible. So sustained success in teaching requires being able to accept the fact that we are never totally successful and that a certain amount of failure is part of the job. In short, we must be able to accept failure without thinking we are failures. It is a crucial dimension of professional judgment.

This aspect of expectancy is important as you implement the suggestions I make in this book. My suggestions are, of course, idealistic. I am arguing for instruction incorporating the best of what we know about effective reading instruction. But, realistically, can you implement all my suggestions in a perfect way in every lesson every day? Of course not. *So a crucially important aspect of professional judgment is the ability to take suggestions such as are provided here, apply them to the extent that you can, and forgive yourself when you are not perfect.*

Both aspects of expectation also apply to implementing Common Core standards. The Common Core itself sets high expectations when they state that every student should achieve every standard at grade level. Such a high expectation is good. You, too, should have high expectations for your students.

But at the same time, you must be realistic. Individual differences are a reality, managing a classroom is complex, and all sorts of variables impact whether or not students meet standards. And while you can improve your chances of having every student meet every standard by implementing what I suggest here, it is unrealistic to expect all students to meet every standard at grade level.

So an important part of being professional is to exercise judgment about yourself and your work. Yes, set high expectations for yourself and your students. You will garner the rewards of teaching when you succeed. But you will not always succeed, and when you don't, you must forgive yourself. In the end, the ability to do so is *key* to sustaining a long and rewarding professional career.

SUMMARY

As stated in the introduction to this chapter, explicit explanations alone are not effective. What makes explicit instruction effective is teachers who impose their will on instructional resources such as those I provide in Part II. Whether it is in teaching generally, or in teaching to the Common Core standards particularly, effective teachers are those who say, "These are suggestions; my job is to adapt them to my situation." So helping struggling readers meet the Common Core standards lies not as much with the explicit explanations I suggest as it does with you being proactive in implementing them professionally.

This is not bad news. It is good news. Teaching would be boring if all we had to do was follow directions mindlessly. It would be technical work, and we would not deserve the label of "professional." Teaching is a profession because effectiveness depends on adjusting, adapting, creating, and molding instruction to different students and to different situations in a context fraught with difficulties. While this book is designed to ease the difficulty of the task, in the end the crucial variable is you and your professionalism.

PART II
THE TEACHING EXAMPLES

EXAMPLES FOR
EXPLAINING LITERATURE

Example 1

Reading for Key Details
(KEY IDEAS AND DETAILS—RL STANDARD 1)

Note: "Reading for Key Details" is a Common Core standard for informational text as well as for literature. The suggestions that follow for assessing and teaching reading for details in literature should also be used when teaching students how to read for details in informational text.

BACKGROUND

The standards for reading for details range in difficulty from "reading to answer questions about key details" at grade 1 to more complex levels of comprehension in higher grades, such as the seventh-grade one illustrated here.

To teach students how to read for details, first ensure there is a statement of purpose. In the following example, for instance, the purpose is to find details supporting a class project. With the purpose firmly in mind, two steps are then required:

1. Readers use their previously learned strategy of predicting–monitoring–repredicting. They think about what they already know, make a prediction about what details will be found, monitor that prediction as they encounter details in the text, and question whether the detail they find fits their prediction or causes them to repredict.

2. They analyze each detail to determine whether or not it supports their purpose.

The example provided here is based on the Common Core's grade 7 standard *RL.7.1: Cite several pieces of textual evidence to support analysis of what the text says.* It assumes a hypothetical seventh-grade situation using adolescent literature.

Note to teachers of other grade levels: The process described here for seventh grade can be adapted for use at other grade levels. For instance, a kindergarten teacher who is reading aloud the big book *Goodnight Moon,* by Margaret Wise Brown (Scholastic, 1947) could teach reading for details as listening comprehension by providing basically the same explanation of noting purpose and then predicting to meet *RL.K.1: With prompting and support, ask and answer questions about key details in a text.*

PRE-LESSON CONSIDERATIONS

Pre-Instruction Assessment

You will know students are not ready to meet the Common Core standard for reading for details if, during discussion of literature, you note students who cannot answer questions about key details and/or cannot answer questions about how details support their purposes.

Large Conceptual Ideas You Can Reinforce during This Lesson

As you teach this lesson, look for opportunities to reinforce big understandings about reading such as the following:

- Comprehension is a proactive endeavor; waiting passively for meaning to arrive does not work.
- Most predictions we make at the beginning need to be modified.
- Almost all comprehension involves a predicting–monitoring–repredicting cycle.
- One must always be conscious of one's purpose in order to comprehend well.
- Reading is empowering because we can use it to achieve purposes important to us.

ORGANIZING FOR INSTRUCTION

Embedding Instruction in Reading for Purpose and Understanding

This example is set in a hypothetical middle school literature class. It assumes the class has been using various pieces of literature to pursue a long-term project about what it means to be human. Currently, the class is reading Sharon Creech's *Walk Two Moons* (Harper Trophy, 1994). Because some students have not met the Common Core standard *RL.7.1*, the teacher forms a small group of those students and uses *Walk Two Moons* to work on reading for key details.

Ideas for Differentiating Instruction

One idea you could use if you were this teacher: Students not working with you on this standard might complete tiered assignments the teacher has previously prepared that involve them further in the project on what it means to be human.

THE LESSON

Post, Display, or State the Objective

"Today we're going to analyze details in *Walk Two Moons* so that we can learn more about what it means to be human. By the end of this lesson, you will be able to describe how you found details in *Walk Two Moons* and how you decided whether these details contribute to our understanding of what it means to be human."

Introducing the Lesson

Say something like:

> "As we read *Walk Two Moons*, we want to be looking for details in the story and whether they help us answer our question about what makes us human. We already know from other stories that love and hurt are associated with being human. So we can use that background knowledge to make an initial prediction. I'm going to show you how to do this as we read the first chapter of *Walk Two Moons*

together. Then, later on, you will show me how you do it. Our goal is to use the details to help us add more to our understanding of what it means to be human."

Stating the Secret to Doing It

Say something like:

> "To do this, you must, first, keep in mind that we're looking for details that contribute to our understanding of what it means to be human; then use your previously learned strategy of predicting–monitoring–repredicting to (1) make a prediction about what details we will find to help answer our questions about what it means to be human; (2) monitor to see whether your prediction is coming true, and if it is, how it helps us with our questions about what it means to be human; and (3) make a new prediction if the details you find are not what you expected or do not help us understand what it means to be human."

Modeling the Thinking

Say something like:

> "We have already talked about the fact that the title and clues following the title page suggest that this story has something to do with what Native Americans say about not judging someone 'until you've walked two moons in his moccasins.' So using that prior knowledge and what we've learned about what it means to be human from other stories we read earlier, I'm going to make a prediction that the key details will tell me something about not making judgments about people. Follow along with me as I begin reading the first chapter. I talk to myself about the first detail—that the girl in the story moved from Kentucky to a new house in Ohio. Immediately, I'm questioning myself, saying, 'This doesn't seem to be a detail about making judgments, and I don't think it will help me understand what it means to be human.
>
> "As I move to the bottom of page 1 and to the top of page 2, I continue monitoring that prediction. The girl seems to be unhappy because of what she says about 'no trees' and 'houses all jammed together.' In my experience, when I talk like that it means I'm unhappy. So I begin changing my prediction. Maybe this is about

problems humans have when they are moving to such a different place.

"But as I read on, I encounter details about a red-haired lady named Margaret. And the girl doesn't want to greet her. It seems like she is rejecting the red-haired woman. That makes me think again about 'walking in someone else's moccasins.' So I change my prediction again. I think maybe the girl is going to find out that she shouldn't judge the red-haired lady. Maybe that will help with our purpose of what makes us human.

"Do you see how I keep talking to myself as I encounter details? I make a prediction, and then I talk to myself about whether that prediction is making sense in terms of my purpose. So now we have a new prediction, but we must see if this prediction results in details that help us understand what it means to be human. So let's read on in Chapter 1 and see if you can do as I did."

Scaffolded Assistance

Level 1: Extensive Teacher Help

Say something like:

> "All right, as we read down to the bottom of page 2, we monitor what is happening and we find there is another detail we should be paying attention to. What is that? Yes, the girl who is telling the story says there is a 'round girl's face' in the upstairs window. Are you asking what that detail has to do with the story? And what it might mean for being human? Does it make you think you should make a new prediction? Yes, maybe this is going to be a story about the friendship between two girls. What could that tell us about being human?"

Level 2: Less Teacher Help

Say something like:

> "All of a sudden, in the next paragraph we encounter a detail about 'being locked in a car with my grandparents.' Are you questioning? What are you saying? Right, this isn't what I expected. But we know we have to make it fit. Are you looking for clues? What do you find? Yes, there are details about the girl telling her grandparents about

Phoebe. But what prediction can we make about this detail and our purpose? What can this have to do with learning what it means to be human?"

Level 3: No Teacher Help

As students become comfortable finding key details, direct them to read the remaining pages in the chapter, to report what details they find and whether these details contribute to their understanding of what it means to be human. By the end of the chapter, they should be questioning the validity of their earlier predictions and should be reporting details that support the idea that you shouldn't judge others until you have "walked in their moccasins."

Continued Application to Reading

As the class moves into subsequent chapters of *Walk Two Moons*, remind students to continue using what they have learned about reading for key details and about analyzing whether those details contribute to the "what it means to be human" project.

POST-LESSON CONSIDERATIONS

Post-Instruction Assessment

To determine whether students are now ready to meet the "reading for key details" standard, watch in subsequent reading activities to see whether students report on the mental self-talk they do when reading for details and when analyzing whether the details have importance in terms of their purpose for reading. For instance, can they describe where their monitoring caused them to pause and reconsider? Do they report questioning themselves about whether their predictions are making sense? And when encountering a detail or set of details that cause them to modify a prediction, can they give examples of how they created a new prediction? And in the end, can they identify details that support their goal of understanding what it means to be human?

Links to Common Core Writing Standards

Good writing requires coherence. But maintaining coherence in writing is one of the most difficult things for young writers to do. They are helped to do this if, when writing, they are conscious of the predicting–monitoring–repredicting cycle used in reading and try to insert into their writing details that help minimize the amount of repredicting their readers will have to do. This is a focus of writing standard *W.7.2b: Develop a topic with relevant facts, definitions, concrete details, quotations, or other information and examples.* Tying the teaching of reading for details to this writing standard helps students meet both the reading and the writing standard.

Example 2

Drawing Inferences

(KEY IDEAS AND DETAILS—RL STANDARD 1)

Note: The Common Core combines "drawing inferences" with "reading for key details" in Standard 1. In this book, however, the two are separated for teaching purposes, with Example 1 providing a sample for how to read for details and this example providing a sample for how to draw inferences.

BACKGROUND

Inferring is the ability to "read between the lines" or to get the meaning an author implies but does not state directly.

As noted in Chapter 2, virtually all comprehension requires inferring. The reader, operating from one set of background experiences, cannot know precisely what the author meant because the author was operating from a different set of background experiences. Comprehension always involves trying to "get inside the author's head" to see what he or she really meant when the text was composed. Even when the author says something straightforward such as "The dress is red," the reader must infer the shade of red, the style of the dress, and so on.

Note: The Common Core lists "drawing inferences" as a standard for Informational Text (RI.1) as well as for literature. When teaching students to draw inferences in informational text, adapt and use this sample lesson.

To teach students how to infer, have them employ their previously learned predicting–monitoring–repredicting cycle in which they use text clues and their own prior knowledge to infer what the author means.

The example provided here is based on the second part of the grade 4 Common Core standard *RL.4.1: Refer to details and examples in a text when explaining what the text says explicitly and when drawing inferences from the text.* It assumes a hypothetical fourth-grade situation.

Note to teachers of other grade levels: The process described here for fourth grade can be adapted for use at other grade levels. For instance, this sample lesson and its suggestions for using the predicting–monitoring–repredicting cycle requires only minor changes when teaching the seventh-grade standard: *RL.7.1: Cite several pieces of textual evidence to support analysis of what the text says explicitly as well as inferences drawn from the text.* Similarly, the suggestions provided here could be applied in a listening situation in first grade in which the teacher reads the big book version of Tomie dePaola's *Mice Squeak, We Speak* (Scholastic, 1998) and teaches inferring as part of that activity.

PRE-LESSON CONSIDERATIONS

Pre-Instruction Assessment

You will know students are not ready to meet a standard for "drawing inferences" if, when reading literature (or informational text), students are unable to answer questions requiring an understanding of what the author has implied but has not stated explicitly.

Large Conceptual Ideas You Can Reinforce during This Lesson

As you teach this lesson, look for opportunities to reinforce big understandings about reading such as the following:

- Authors often leave information unstated or implied, expecting the reader to infer it.
- Authors compose text based on their background experience, and we construct meanings based on what the author's words make us think about (i.e., our experiences with those words).

- As comprehenders, we are always inferring, even when we are predicting.
- Comprehension is a process of building meaning—we cannot wait for meaning to come to us.
- Reading literature is enriching because it helps us to understand people and problems in life.

ORGANIZING FOR INSTRUCTION

Embedding Instruction in Reading for Purpose and Understanding

This example assumes a fourth-grade class in which the teacher uses a workshop structure, with members of the class divided into several literature groups, with each group reading a different novel. The goal for all the groups is, after finishing their novels, to conduct a whole-group discussion on whether their novels were "enriching" in the sense of helping them better understand people and human problems. This example focuses on the group reading E. L. Konigsburg's *The View from Saturday* (Scholastic, 1996). The members of the group have difficulty grasping meanings implied by the author. The teacher decides to teach a lesson on how to infer and to then have students apply that strategy in the next chapter of *The View from Saturday.*

Ideas for Differentiating Instruction

One idea you could use if you were this teacher: Students not working with you on this standard continue to work in their literature circles in the workshop structure. In their groups, students are either reading their novels or are discussing in pairs whether the novel "enriched" them.

THE LESSON

Post, Display, or State the Objective

"By the end of this lesson, you will be able to state information E. L. Konigsburg has not directly stated but, instead, has inserted 'between the lines' of *The View from Saturday.*"

Introducing the Lesson

Say something like:

> "We have been reading *The View from Saturday*, and at the end we are going to be discussing with the other groups whether our novel is 'enriching' in any way. Sometimes, what is 'enriching' about a novel is not stated directly but is implied by the author—that is, you have to be able to 'read between the lines' in order to get the meaning. I'm going to show you how to 'read between the lines' today using some sentences I made up in which I've implied, but not stated, meaning I want you to get. When we have done that and understand how to draw inferences, we'll read the next chapter in *The View from Saturday* and you will have an opportunity to use what we learned today."

Stating the Secret to Doing It

Say something like:

> "The secret to 'reading between the lines' is to note the clue words the author uses and then to use your background knowledge about those words and the predicting–monitoring–repredicting cycle to predict what the author is implying—that is, what is being said 'between the lines.'"

Modeling the Thinking

Say something like:

> "Let me show you how I figure out meaning that is not directly stated by the author. Let's use an example like the following [displays the following on chart paper]:
>
> > The sky was dark and the fog blocked out everything. I couldn't see 3 feet in front of me. I didn't know which way to turn. I was frozen to the spot.
>
> "The author wants me to get a certain feeling here, but doesn't want to state it directly. So I have to put myself in this character's place and use my own experience to draw an inference. What I do is say

to myself, 'If it were me who was out on a dark and foggy night and didn't know which way to turn, how would that make me feel?' If it were me, it would make me feel scared. And if I would be scared in that situation, that is probably how the character in the story feels too. So that is the prediction I make. Even though the author hasn't said the character was scared, I predict that she is scared based on how the author's words make me feel. I did it by thinking about how I would feel in that situation, and I used that to predict that the author wanted me to feel like that. Now I will read on and monitor that prediction to see if it holds up. If clues that come later are different, I can change my prediction."

Scaffolded Assistance

Level 1: Extensive Teacher Help

Say something like:

> "Let's look at another example together and see if we can figure out what the author wants us to think even though it doesn't say so directly [displays the following on chart paper]:
>
>> When the teacher praised her for the good job she did, Mildred lowered her eyes and blushed. She said, "Oh, it was nothing. Anybody could have done it." When the teacher continued to praise her, Mildred got even more red in the face.
>
> "The author is implying something here about the kind of person Mildred is. So how are we going to figure out what the author wants us to think about Mildred? Does the author give some clues? Yes, she says that, when praised, Mildred lowers her eyes, blushes, and gets red in the face. Those are clues the author wants us to use to figure out what the author means, even though she doesn't say it directly. To figure out what she means, we have to think about our own experience with people who, when praised, lower their eyes, blush, and get red in the face. Have you ever known someone like that? So how would you describe that person? Yes, some people act like that when they are embarrassed. So because in our experience we have known persons who get embarrassed when they are complimented, we predict that this is what the author wants us to think. If we get different

clues about Mildred's actions when we read on, we can change that prediction."

Level 2: Less Teacher Help

Say something like:

"Now let's try another example. But this time I won't give you as much help. You must do more of the thinking yourselves. I'm just going to ask questions to point you in the right direction. Remember the secret for doing this: first, look for clues the author provides, then think about your own experience with those clues and, on the basis of your experience, predict what meaning the author is implying. Here's the example [displays the following]:

> The team boarded the school bus and started out for the big game.
> If they won this game, they would be champions! Suddenly, 15
> miles from the site of the game, the bus broke down. There they
> sat, waiting. Nobody seemed to know what to do, and it was getting
> closer and closer to game time.

"In this example, the author doesn't tell you what the players are feeling. Instead, the author assumes you will figure it out for yourselves. So what do we do to figure out what the author is implying here? Are there clues? And can you think of experiences you've had that were similar in some way? How did you feel in those situations? If that is how you felt, can you predict how the team players in this example were feeling?"

Level 3: No Teacher Help

Once students demonstrate confidence in inferring, you might want to use an example from *The View from Saturday*. But now you provide very little help. For instance, you might say:

"Okay, now let's look at an example in the story we're reading in our literature circle. Read the first paragraph in Chapter 3, where the principal, Margaret Draper, is being described. Read the paragraph to yourselves. E .L. Konigsburg doesn't come right out and tell us what kind of principal Margaret Draper was, but she gives us clues and wants us to figure it out for ourselves. Look for those clues and use your own experience to decide what kind of principal she was. Remember that I am going to ask you to tell me how you figured it out, so be aware of the thinking you are doing as you use the strategy."

Continued Application to Reading

This example illustrates how you might teach a standard and then apply it to a text selection. The teacher will continue to monitor students' application of the standard as they read other chapters in *The View from Saturday*, as well as other reading situations.

POST-LESSON CONSIDERATIONS

Post-Instruction Assessment

You will know students are ready to meet the Common Core standard for drawing inferences if, during discussions of literature, they are able to answer questions about what authors implied in the text.

Links to Common Core Writing Standards

The fourth-grade writing standards include the following: *W.4.3d: Use concrete words and phrases and sensory details to convey experiences and events precisely.* Some "experiences and events" are conveyed explicitly and some are implied. When teaching students to meet this writing standard, what they have learned about inferring meaning when reading can be used to help them learn to imply meaning when conveying "experiences and events" in their writing.

Example 3

Theme

(KEY IDEAS AND DETAILS—RL STANDARD 2)

BACKGROUND

Theme is the "big idea" in a piece of literature. When authors write stories, poems, or plays, they usually have a message to convey about life, living, or humanity. Sometimes the theme is the moral of a story, with *Aesop's Fables* being prominent examples of explicitly stated themes. More typically, however, the theme in literature is implied. For this reason, theme is often difficult to identify. The reader must think across the whole story to figure it out.

Despite this difficulty, theme is crucially important if students are to learn to appreciate literature. While stories, poems, and plays can be read purely for enjoyment, the best literature endures because it conveys a lasting message. Readers who understand that literature can convey important "big ideas," and who have a strategy for figuring out what the theme is, can not only enjoy literature but also profit from it.

> To teach students to identify theme, first establish the expectation that good readers of literature look beyond the surface enjoyment of the story or poem or play to the deeper meaning the author may be conveying. Then students must identify details such as how characters respond, make a prediction about what "big idea" the author might be conveying, employ the predicting–monitoring–repredicting cycle to modify the prediction as needed, and look at the details collectively to determine what the theme might be and how the story or poem or play could be summarized.

The teaching example provided here is based on the grade 5 Common Core standard *RL.5.2: Determine a theme of a story, drama, or poem from details in the text, including how characters in a story or drama respond to challenges or how the speaker in a poem reflects upon a topic; summarize the text.* It assumes a hypothetical fifth-grade classroom.

Note to teachers of other grade levels: This example can be adapted and used when teaching to a second-grade standard such as *RL.2.2: Recount stories, including fables and folktales from diverse cultures, and determine their central message, or moral.* The teacher could use the book *Just Not Quite Right*, by Susan Ulrich Olsen (Mindset Press, 2000), and explain the same process of identifying clues in the details and using one's background experience to predict central messages.

PRE-LESSON CONSIDERATIONS

Pre-Instruction Assessment

You will know students are not ready to meet the standard for determining "theme" if, when discussing stories, poems, or drama with students, they show no understanding that literature conveys messages that go beyond the story line itself or cannot summarize the text by identifying a "big message" the author may be conveying.

Large Conceptual Ideas You Can Reinforce during This Lesson

As you teach this lesson, look for opportunities to reinforce big understandings about reading such as the following:

- Stories and poems are fun to read, but authors also have "big ideas" or "themes" they want to convey about life and living.
- Determining theme, as with much of comprehension, requires proactive questioning of the author.
- All comprehension, including theme, is an *interpretation* based on the reader's background experience; therefore, different people may see different themes in a particular story or poem.
- Analysis of the meaning in literature often requires that ideas be combined together, or categorized.
- Identifying theme in literature helps us understand humans and human problems.

ORGANIZING FOR INSTRUCTION

Embedding Instruction in Reading for Purpose and Understanding

This example is set in a fifth grade where the teacher has partnered each of her fifth graders with a younger student in a lower grade. The task is to write stories that contain a message, or a theme, and to ultimately read those stories to their younger students. In preparation for developing an understanding of theme, the teacher has orally read to the class Tom Birdseye's *Just Call Me Stupid* (Holiday House, 1993). The teacher is now taking a small group of students who have not yet met the standard back through that story in order to model how to meet the standard for theme.

Ideas for Differentiating Instruction

One idea you could use if you were this teacher: Students not working with you on this standard work individually on writing their own stories for their younger friends.

THE LESSON

Display, Post, or State the Objective

"By the end of this lesson, you will be able to state what an author's theme might be for the story we just finished reading and will be able to describe the thinking you did to determine the theme."

Introducing the Lesson

Say something like:

> "We just finished reading *Just Call Me Stupid*. It was a great story. But the author was also trying to convey a 'big idea'—he wants us to understand something important about life or living that goes beyond just what happens in the story. When you write your stories for your young friends, you too will tell a story, but you will also try to include in the story a big idea you want your younger friends to understand about living and life. We call these big ideas 'themes.' I'm going to show you how I do this in the first sections of the book. Then you will do it with the later sections of the book."

Stating the Secret to Doing It

Say something like:

> "It is difficult to identify themes because authors seldom state the theme; instead, we have to look across the whole story and infer it. As we read along we have to pay attention to details such as how a character is feeling or how a character is responding in the story and make a prediction about what the theme might be, using our monitoring and repredicting skills to change our prediction if we need to. Then we have to repeat that for other details we encounter later. Finally, we look across all those story details and combine them together to determine the theme for the story."

Modeling the Thinking

Say something like:

> "Let me show you how I do it. Look at Chapter 1 [projects it on the white board/smart board]. You'll remember that in the very first paragraph the teacher scolds Patrick because, even though he's a fifth grader, he doesn't know how to read [uses a laser pointer to indicate the sentence and does the same in the passages that follow]. As I read along, I note that Patrick feels he is stupid. I can use this detail and my own experience to predict how Patrick is feeling. I think he must be feeling terrible about himself. This may be a clue to the author's theme, so I keep that prediction in mind as I read along. When I get to Chapter 2 [teacher projects this chapter on the white board/smart board], I find that Patrick's father, who doesn't live with him anymore, calls him stupid, even though his mother seems to believe in him. These details are clues that may help me figure out the theme—it seems that Patrick feels bad because lots of people think he is stupid, even if his Mom doesn't. Now I need to combine these two ideas together [links the two ideas on the white board/smart board]. I ask myself, 'What do these two details seem to be saying about what the author wants me to think is the big idea?' When I do that, I use my own experience. In my experience, when something like this happens I think the author is saying you feel bad when you can't read and when lots of people around you do not support you.

"Did you see how I combined details about the characters and my own experience to make a prediction about what the theme might be? Now I must monitor that prediction as I read Chapters 3 and 4 and see if it needs to be changed."

Scaffolded Assistance

Level 1: Extensive Teacher Help

Say something like:

"Okay, let's look at Chapters 3 and 4, but now you have to help me [projects those chapters on the white board/smart board]. We have to keep in mind our first prediction about the theme as we identify new details and combine them together. In Chapter 3, we find that Patrick has created a 'kingdom' in his backyard. What does your experience make you think about why Patrick does that? Yes, maybe Patrick is trying to find a place where he can feel good about himself. So can we combine this prediction with the one we made before [uses the white board/smart board to visually link the two ideas]? Yes, even though Patrick feels bad, he is trying to do something to feel good. Now let's go to Chapter 4. What happens in Chapter 4, and how can you use your experience to predict what the author is telling us about his theme? Yes, Patrick is getting picked on at school, but look at how he is responding [points with the laser pointer]. He's making himself feel better by drawing. So let's combine this detail about Patrick with the ones we have already [displays the two details]. When we do that, we see two ways Patrick is finding ways to feel good even though he can't read. So what can we predict, using our own experience, about the theme? Yes, maybe it has something to do with Patrick finding ways to feel good about himself even though he can't read well."

Level 2: Less Teacher Help

Say something like:

"Now let's look at the details about what happens in Chapters 5 and 6 [teacher projects these]. What is an important detail in Chapter 5? Yes, he finds a friend and he plays chess. And then in Chapter 6 we find that his friend helps him feel good about his ability to play chess and to draw. So what is the message here? Yes, his friend is pointing out Patrick's strong points. Can we combine that detail with our earlier predictions without me displaying the details as I did before? We know from our earlier predictions that Patrick felt bad about himself but was trying to do things to make himself feel better. What has now changed? Can we use our experience to make a new prediction? Yes, it seems that now there is someone in addition to his mom who thinks Patrick is smart. So when we combine our predictions together, what can we say? Yes, perhaps the theme has something to do with the importance of having someone who sees what your strong points are."

Level 3: No Teacher Help

The teacher continues projecting the story chapter by chapter, and students identify the details and combine them to decide on a theme. Ultimately, they combine all their predictions together and develop the overall theme for the book—that success is often tied to having a good friend who believes in you and helps you believe in yourself.

Continued Application to Reading

Identifying theme is difficult. It usually requires much repetition before students become comfortable inferring what big message authors are conveying. Consequently, in addition to applying what they have learned in *Just Call Me Stupid*, the teacher will look for opportunities on subsequent days to have students apply this strategy to reading other stories, poems, or plays.

POST-LESSON CONSIDERATIONS

Post-Instruction Assessment

You will know students are ready to meet the standard for "theme" if, when discussing literature on subsequent days, students identify details they used and how they combined them to identify a theme that summarizes the piece of literature.

Links to Common Core Writing Standards

The Common Core writing standards for grade 5 include the following: *W.5.3e: Provide a conclusion that follows from the narrated experiences and events.* In writing as in reading, students should be encouraged to have the "narrated experiences and events" contribute to an overall theme. Transferring to writing what students have learned about theme in reading will help strengthen both their reading and the writing skills.

Example 4

Character Traits and Motivations

(KEY IDEAS AND DETAILS—RL STANDARD 3)

BACKGROUND

Literature is full of characters. Characters move the action along. Consequently, in order to comprehend literature well, one must be able to identify the traits and motivations of characters.

> To teach students to identify character traits and motivations, begin by making them aware that authors invent both story characters and their traits and motivations, and that the author then uses those characters' traits and motivations to influence what happens in stories. Once that understanding is in place, readers use the predicting–monitoring–repredicting strategy to identify character traits and motivations and how characters are moving the story forward.

The teaching example that follows is based on the Common Core's second-grade standard *RL.2.3: Describe how characters in a story respond to major events and challenges.* It assumes a hypothetical second-grade classroom.

> *Note for teachers of other grade levels:* You can adapt the following suggestions to your particular situation. For instance, fifth or sixth graders reading Gary Larson's *There's a Hair in My Dirt* (HarperCollins, 1998) can similarly be taught to expect authors to use characters in intentional ways in the

84

stories they write and can then use their predicting–monitoring–repredicting skills to identify characters' traits and motivations and how they influenced story events.

PRE-LESSON CONSIDERATIONS

Pre-Instruction Assessment

You will know students are not ready to meet the standard for "character traits and motivation" if, when reading stories to the class or when students are reading stories on their own, they cannot answer questions about how characters' actions influence what happens in the story, and they cannot describe traits or motivations that may have caused characters to act as they did.

Large Conceptual Ideas You Can Reinforce during This Lesson

As you teach this lesson, look for opportunities to reinforce big understandings about reading such as the following:

- Readers expect stories to have characters and expect that authors of stories give characters certain traits and motivations that will influence story events.
- Like much of comprehension, determining character traits and motivations requires readers to infer what meaning the author intends.
- Reading and writing have much in common, and what we learn about characters in reading can be used when we write stories having characters.
- Understanding characters in stories help us understand people's behavior.

ORGANIZING FOR INSTRUCTION

Embedding Instruction in Reading for Purpose and Understanding

This example is set in a second-grade classroom. The teacher has initiated a unit in which students are writing stories they will then contribute to the room library. She chooses to read aloud to the class Daniel Kirk's *Library Mouse* (Abrams Books, 2007). She does so two times. First, she reads it to make the point that all the students can be writers of stories.

But she then also uses the *Library Mouse* the next day to teach the standard for character traits and motivation to those students who have not yet met that standard.

Ideas for Differentiating Instruction

One idea you could use if you were this teacher: Students not working with you on this standard continue to work on stories they are writing for the school library.

THE LESSON

Display, Post, or State the Objective

"By the end of this lesson, you will be able to identify how the characters in *Library Mouse* influenced major events in the story and the traits or motivations that caused the characters to do what they did."

Introducing the Lesson

Say something like:

> "Yesterday, we heard the story in which Sam, the mouse, tricked kids into becoming story writers with his hidden 'meet the author' mirror. Today, let's look at this story again, but this time let's look at how the author has story characters influence events in the story, and what that tells us about the characters' traits and motivations. It's important for readers to be able to do this in order to fully understand the story. But it is even more important for us as writers, because we are going to have characters in our stories and we will want to give them traits and motivations that will cause certain story events to happen."

Stating the Secret to Doing It

Say something like:

> "To be able to identify character traits and motivations, you must start from the understanding that authors invent characters and give those characters certain traits and motivations so that, as the story progresses, the author can influence story events by having his

characters take certain actions. If you understand that, then as you read along in the story you will be alert for events triggered by characters, and you will use your predicting–monitoring–repredicting skills to identify those events and to identify how and why characters triggered those events."

Modeling the Thinking

Say something like:

> "Let me show you how I do it. When we start reading *Library Mouse*, I am alert for how characters influence events. This story starts out on pages 1 and 2 with Sam the mouse being quite happy. Given details such as Sam living alone behind the reference stacks of the library and thinking to himself that 'life is very good indeed,' I can predict that he is a very happy mouse. That is one character trait he has. But he doesn't yet seem to be influencing story events. So I read on, keeping in mind my prediction that he's a happy mouse but also looking to see if he is going to influence events.
>
> "On pages 3 and 4, I learn that he is a reader himself and that he reads almost everything. Now I have to modify my prediction about Sam. Not only is he happy, but he must be smart too, because I know from my own experience that learning to read is not always easy. So the fact that he is smart is another character trait. But I don't see yet if his traits and motivations are influencing events. So let's read on.
>
> "On pages 5, 6, and 7 I find out that Sam has decided to write a book of his own. And not only that, he stuck the book he wrote about his own life into the biography/autobiography section of the library. So I think about this new detail and begin to ask myself questions. In my experience, what kind of person writes a book, puts it on a shelf, and then goes home and waits? I think I need to make a better prediction about what kind of person Sam is. It makes me think, from my experience background, that he is mischievous. And I bet what he does will influence what happens in the story. In fact, I predict someone is going to find Sam's story.
>
> "Do you see how I started out with the expectation that the story character will have certain traits, and how I used my experience background to predict what those traits might be, and how Sam's actions might influence story events? So let's see if we can try making a prediction together."

Scaffolded Assistance

Level 1: Extensive Teacher Help

Say something like:

> "What's happening on page 8? Yes, they find Sam's book about him-
> self. And the librarian shows it to the other librarians. How do you
> suppose the librarian feels? Let's use our experience: If we were in
> her place and we found this book, how would we feel? Yes, we'd
> probably feel strange or funny. We'd think this was a mystery. So
> can you predict what she'll do now? How will she influence the next
> events in the story? Yes, we expect that she'll do something to try to
> find out who wrote this book."

Level 2: Less Teacher Help

Say something like:

> "Okay, what do we find as we read on? Yes, we find out that appar-
> ently the librarian is not doing something to find out who wrote the
> book. Instead, we find that Sam is writing another book and the
> librarian is showing the book to children at story time. Hmmm, so
> what do you think our characters will do next? Can you make a pre-
> diction about what Sam will do? About what the librarian will do?
> Now we see that Sam is writing a chapter book. Are we still predict-
> ing that he is smart and mischievous? Okay, maybe we have to add
> to our prediction that Sam is a bit sneaky because the author says
> Sam 'sneakily' placed his book on the shelf. And what is the librarian
> doing? Yes, she's writing a note to Sam inviting him to class. How do
> you think this will influence the events of the story? Do you have a
> prediction?"

Level 3: No Teacher Help

The teacher continues leading a class discussion on the events in *Library
Mouse* and how Sam's responses to the librarian's note ultimately leads to
all the students writing stories of their own.

Continued Application to Reading

Students will apply what they have learned about character traits and motivations in the stories they are writing. Additionally, the teacher will look for opportunities for students to apply the strategy in other literature they will be reading.

POST-LESSON CONSIDERATIONS

Post-Instruction Assessment

You will know students are ready to meet the standard for "character traits and motivations" if you observe the students as they finish reading *Library Mouse* or after reading other stories and see that they are able to answer questions about characters, their actions, and their motivations and how characters influenced story events.

Links to Common Core Writing Standards

When writing stories, students should invent characters possessing character traits and motivations that help develop the action in the story. This is reflected in writing standard *W.3.3b: Use dialogue and description of actions, thoughts, and feelings to develop experiences or show the responses of characters to situations.* Integrating the teaching of character traits in reading with the teaching of character traits in writing makes it easier for students to become stronger in both reading and writing. For instance, in the example just provided in which students are writing their own stories, the teacher will remind them to invent story characters whose traits and motivations will influence the major events in the story.

Example 5

Descriptive Words and Phrases
(CRAFT AND STRUCTURE—RL STANDARD 4)

BACKGROUND

The Common Core includes several vocabulary standards. This one focuses on nonliteral words and phrases that appeal to the senses and help readers generate images. Descriptive language is particularly important in literature because it is often the sensory images that make stories vibrant and alive. Readers see what the characters see, hear what the characters hear, and feel what the characters feel. These emotional responses are often what "hook" students and cause them to think reading is "cool."

> To teach students to interpret descriptive language, have them use prior knowledge to predict. In this case, readers use what they know about a particular descriptive word or phrase and what it makes them think. They then use that to predict the image the author intends to convey, monitor that prediction, and repredict as needed.

The example provided here is based on the grade 1 Common Core standard *RL.1.4: Identify words and phrases in stories or poems that suggest feelings or appeal to the senses.* It assumes a hypothetical first-grade *listening* situation.

> *Note for teachers of other grade levels:* Descriptive language appears in narrative text at all levels and can be taught in reading as well as listening, using much the same explanation as described here. For instance, fifth

or sixth graders reading Natalie Babbitt's *Tuck Everlasting* (Bantam Dell, 1975) will encounter passages having descriptive phrases in which a road is described as "a pleasant tangent" that "ambled down." They can be taught to similarly use "picture words" and their background knowledge to predict what emotion the author is trying to convey.

PRE-LESSON CONSIDERATIONS

Pre-Instruction Assessment

You will know students are not ready to meet the standard for descriptive words and phrases if, when reading stories to students or when students are reading stories themselves, you observe that they are not emotionally involved. When questioned, they cannot tell you how the story made them feel; nor can they describe what they heard or saw in their minds as they were reading.

Large Conceptual Understandings You Can Reinforce during This Lesson

As you teach this lesson, look for opportunities to reinforce several large understandings about reading such as the following:

* Comprehension requires proactive effort.
* When authors write stories, they want us to be emotionally involved in the story.
* Understanding an author's message requires careful analysis of the words and phrases the author uses.
* Reading and writing are reciprocal processes.

ORGANIZING FOR INSTRUCTION

Embedding Instruction in Reading for Purpose and Understanding

This example is set in a first-grade classroom. It assumes that a day earlier the teacher had orally read Jane Yolen's *Owl Moon* (Scholastic, 1987) as part of a class project on "What makes stories fun?" Because the teacher has assessed that some students are not responding to descriptive language, the teacher wants to use the same book today to develop that ability with that small group of students. She teaches it as a *listening* comprehension lesson because these students have not yet learned to read well enough to read *Owl Moon* on their own.

Ideas for Differentiating Instruction

One idea you could use if you were this teacher: Students not working with you on this standard select a task from the "Choice Board" and work in pairs to complete the task.

THE LESSON

Display, Post, or State the Objective

"By the end of this lesson, you will be able to tell what you see and hear and feel as you hear stories like *Owl Moon,* and you will be able to tell how certain words made you feel a certain way or made you see, hear, or smell certain things."

Introducing the Lesson

Say something like:

> "Yesterday I read *Owl Moon* to you, and we really enjoyed learning about going owling. It is a good example of a fun story. Today we are going to use *Owl Moon* again, but this time we are going to use it to further answer our question about what makes stories fun. One of the things that makes stories fun is the descriptive language that helps us make pictures in our minds so that we can see and hear and feel what is happening in the story. I'm going to show you how I build those pictures in my mind using certain words on the first few pages of *Owl Moon.* Pay close attention because, as we move through *Owl Moon,* I will be asking you to show me how *you* build pictures in your minds using the words you hear the author using and how that helps make reading fun."

Stating the Secret to Doing It

Say something like:

> "The secret to building pictures in your mind is to identify the 'picture words' the author uses, and then to think about what those words make you see or hear or feel. If the words make you see or hear or feel in certain ways, then that is probably the picture the author wants you to get."

Modeling the Thinking

Say something like:

> "Listen while I reread the first page of *Owl Moon* so that I can show you how I make pictures in my mind using the author's words. Right here on the first page it says, 'The trees stood still as giant statues' [uses a laser pointer to highlight those words on the white board/ smart board]. Here's a place where the author is using words to help you make a picture in your mind. When she says the trees were like 'giant statues,' she is trying to get me to picture the trees the way she is seeing them. To see them the way she wants me to, I have to think about what I know about statues. I have experience with statues. I know that they are usually really big, and that they don't move at all because they are made of stone. So the picture I'd have of the trees would be that they are big and that they don't move.
>
> "Let's try another place on the same page. The author says that 'Somewhere behind us a train whistle blew, long and low, like a sad, sad song' [uses a laser pointer to indicate on the white board/smart board the lines she is reading]. Here the author is trying to get us to *hear* something, not *see* something. And she wants us to hear it like she hears it, so she uses certain picture words. I have to think of what I know about those picture words. She says the whistle is 'long and low' like a 'sad, sad song.' So I think, 'What do the words *long and low* and *sad song* make me think?' My experience with those words makes me predict that the author wants me to hear sounds that are stretched out and sad-sounding, not happy. See how my experience with the picture words the author uses can help me predict what the author wants me to see and hear?"

Scaffolded Assistance

Level 1: Extensive Teacher Help

Say something like:

> "Let's see if we can create a picture in our minds together. On the next page, the author says, 'A farm dog answered the train, and then a second dog joined in. They sang out, train and dogs, for a real long time' [uses a laser pointer to indicate the words she is reading on the page projected on the white board/smart board]. Is the author trying to get us to see something here or to hear something? Yes, she wants us to hear something the same way she hears it. What words does the author use that helps us hear what she wants us to hear? Yes, she used the words *sang out* to describe what the dogs were doing. Do we have experience with dogs 'singing out' that we could use to predict what the author wants us to hear? Have you heard dogs 'singing out?' Okay, then you can use that experience to hear in your mind what the author wants you to hear at that point in *Owl Moon*. What does it sound like?"

Level 2: Less Teacher Help

Say something like:

> "If we go on to the next page, we find the author saying, 'Our feet crunched over the crisp snow. . . . ' Is the author trying to get you to picture it in a certain way? Yes, she may be trying to get us to hear it like she hears it. Does she give you picture words you can use? Yes, *crunched* and *crisp* can both help us picture what it sounds like because you can use your own experience with 'crunchy' and 'crisp' snow to predict what the author wants you to hear. So what does it sound like? And you know that because that's the way snow sounds to you when it is 'crunchy' and 'crisp'."

Level 3: No Teacher Help

As students get better at picking out descriptive words and phrases and using their experience to create pictures in their minds, read some of the later parts of the book to them and have them describe the images they are creating and how they are using their experience to do it.

Continued Application to Reading

In this example the strategy is taught in a listening situation and is developed after reading the text the day before. But continued application will occur on subsequent days when, in pursuit of their project about "what makes reading fun," the teacher reads different stories to the students and, eventually, when these first graders begin reading stories on their own. The focus continues to be on identifying descriptive words and phrases and then using experience with those to create pictures in the mind.

POST-LESSON CONSIDERATIONS

Post-Instruction Assessment

You will know students are ready to meet the standard for descriptive words and phrases if, in subsequent listening and reading situations, students show greater emotional involvement in stories by demonstrating excitement or sadness or scariness, depending on what is happening. Further, when asked, they should be able to identify the descriptive language they have used to predict what the author wants them to see or hear or feel.

Links to Common Core Writing Standards

The Common Core specifies a writing standard for the primary grades as follows: *W.2.3: Write narratives in which they recount a well-elaborated event or short sequence of events, include details to describe actions, thoughts, and feelings, use temporal words to signal event order, and provide a sense of closure.* The part of this writing standard that focuses on "describing actions, thoughts, and feelings" is closely related to the reading standard for descriptive words and phrases. When teaching this writing standard, it is helpful to encourage students to reverse the descriptive language process. Rather than thinking of descriptive words from the standpoint of a reader trying to figure out what the author is trying to get us to see or hear or feel, students should be encouraged to think about it as a writer who is trying to get a reader to see or hear or feel in certain ways, and therefore chooses to use certain descriptive words and phrases.

Example 6

Text Types

(CRAFT AND STRUCTURE—RL STANDARD 5)

BACKGROUND

Authors write a variety of different kinds of texts. Some write informational text; some write literature. Within each of these larger categories, there are subcategories. In literature, for instance, there are stories, poems, and drama.

Comprehension is enhanced when readers are conscious of the type of text being read. The particular text characteristics cue readers to meaning. For instance, readers of literature expect to find characters, a problem, and a resolution of the problem, and good readers look for them as they read; readers of informational text expect factual information and look for it as they read.

> To teach text types, do much the same as when directly teaching the meaning of new words (see Example 13). Explanation focuses on identifying the features that distinguish the text type.

The teaching example provided here is based on Common Core standard *RL.1.5: Explain major differences between books that tell stories and books that give information, drawing on a wide reading of a range of text types.* It assumes a first-grade situation.

> *Note to teachers of other grade levels:* The same process of identifying distinguishing features of text can be applied to other grade levels. For instance, these suggestions and the same process of focusing on distinguishing

features can be used when teaching to the fifth-grade standard *RL.5.4: Explain major differences between poems, drama, and prose, and refer to the structural elements of poems (e.g., verse, rhythm, meter) and drama (e.g., casts of characters, settings, descriptions, dialogue, stage directions) when writing or speaking about a text.*

PRE-LESSON CONSIDERATIONS

Pre-Instruction Assessment

You will know students are not ready to meet the standard for "text types" if, when you present them with a variety of text types, they are unable to identify which books tell stories and which books give information.

Large Conceptual Ideas You Can Reinforce during This Lesson

As you teach this lesson, look for opportunities to reinforce big understandings about reading such as the following:

- Authors have a purpose for writing; sometimes it is to convey information and sometimes it is to tell a story.
- Reading and writing are reciprocal; what we do in reading is reflected in what we do in writing.
- Good readers and writers know what kind of text they are working with, and they keep the features of that kind of text in mind whether they are reading or writing.

ORGANIZING FOR INSTRUCTION

Embedding Instruction in Reading for Purpose and Understanding

In this hypothetical first-grade situation, the "show-and-tell" session included a student who reported seeing a family of loons on a weekend vacation with her family. Because loons are solitary creatures, the student's report was sparse, consisting primarily of how hard it was for her to observe them. This fact generated considerable interest among the other members of the class, with questions arising about how loons lived, where they had come from, whether they were endangered, and so on. The teacher took this opportunity to provide them with three different types of text and to teach them about text types. She has determined that the entire class needs to meet this standard, so this is a whole-class lesson.

Ideas for Differentiating Instruction

One idea you could use if you were this teacher: Initially, this is a whole-class lesson. But subsequent to this lesson, the teacher's post-instruction assessment will indicate that some students need additional help. For that follow-up lesson, students not working with you are working in cooperative groups using the same three types of text and listing the information they discover about loons for reporting to the class later in the day.

THE LESSON

Display, Post, or State the Objective

"By the end of this lesson, you will have more information about loons, but you will also be able to tell me whether a text is primarily written to tell a story or whether it is primarily written to provide information."

Introducing the Lesson

Say something like:

> "Because you have shown so much interest in loons, I have gathered together three different sources for learning about loons. We will use these to learn more about loons, but I will also show you how to tell whether a text is primarily for giving information or primarily for telling a story."

Stating the Secret to Doing It

Say something like:

> "To tell whether a text is an informational text or a story, we have to pay attention to its features. Informational text has certain features and if we know what they are we can identify an informational text when we see it. Similarly, stories have certain features, and if we know what they are we can identify a story when we see it."

Modeling the Thinking

Say something like:

> "Let me show you how I know the difference between stories and information text. Let's look first at the Wikipedia entry on our computer. If I put in a search for 'loons,' I get the site you see here [brings up the Wikipedia website on her computer and projects it on her white board/smart board]. I can tell this is informational text because the page is full of facts. There's information about loons' size, and color and where they live. It is all facts. That tells me it is written primarily for information.
>
> "Now let's look at this book. It is called *Looking for Loons* (by Jennifer Lloyd; Simply Read Books, 2007) [projects the book]. When we look at the first page and the second page, we see it is about a boy. He is on his porch and is looking for something. And then his parents come out and they talk together. I can tell this is a storybook because there are characters, and they talk to each other.
>
> "So I can tell when a text is informational text because it contains mainly facts, and I can tell when a text is a story because it has characters and talking."

Scaffolded Assistance

Level 1: Extensive Teacher Help

Say something like:

> "Now let's look at two other kinds of text and see if we can tell which is informational and which is a story. Let's look first at a website I found [goes to *www.Biokids.umich.edu*, brings up a section on loons, and projects it on her white board/smart board for the whole class to see]. What do we see here that helps us decide whether this is information or story? Do we see lots of facts? Yes. Do we see any characters or any dialogue? No. So it is informational text because it provides mainly facts, and does not have characters."

Level 2: Less Teacher Help

Say something like:

> "Okay, now let's look at three other texts and see whether they are informational or a story. Here's the first one [holds up *Loon Summer*, by Sandy Gillum; Field Notes Press, 2008]. Are there clues here that tell us whether it is informational or a story? Yes, we see lots of facts here about how loons are good parents. It's all facts. So what kind of text is it? Yes, it's information. Now let's look at another text [holds up *The Legend of the Loon*, by Kathy-jo Wargin; Sleeping Bear Press, 2000]. What do we see when we leaf through the pages of this book? Yes, there are characters, such as Grandmother Lom and her two grandchildren. And is there dialogue? Yes. So what kind of text must this be? Yes, this is a story."

Level 3: No Teacher Help

As the children continue looking through the texts provided by the teacher, they should be looking for the features that distinguish informational texts from stories. For instance, when they encounter the book *Loons* (by George K. Peck; Child's World, 1998), they should immediately categorize it as information because of the prevalence of facts.

Continued Application to Reading

On subsequent days and while pursuing other topics in which a variety of text is available, students should be expected to identify informational text and stories and tell how they distinguish the difference.

POST-LESSON CONSIDERATIONS

Post-Instruction Assessment

You will know students are ready to meet the standard for "text types" if, as noted above, the students successfully identify informational books and stories during subsequent instructional activities.

Links to Common Core Writing Standards

The Common Core standards for writing specify that first graders should be composing both informational and narrative texts. Learning to distinguish informational and story texts in reading will be enhanced if they are integrated with writing of informational text and stories.

Example 7

Story Structure

(CRAFT AND STRUCTURE—RL STANDARD 5)

BACKGROUND

All well-written literature has an internal structure. Stories have an internal structure; poems have an internal structure; drama has an internal structure. Knowing what the structure is, and anticipating it as one reads, aids in comprehension.

Story structure is often referred to as a "story map." It begins with a description of the setting, the problem, and the characters, then describes a series of events, and concludes with a resolution of the problem.

> To teach story structure, start by establishing that all well-written literature has an internal structure. Then be explicit about what the structure is, and help students keep the structure in mind as they use the predicting–monitoring–repredicting cycle to comprehend story meaning.

The example provided here is based on the second-grade Common Core standard *RL.2.5: Describe the overall structure of a story, including how the beginning introduces the story and the ending concludes the action.* It is situated in a hypothetical second-grade classroom.

> *Note for teachers of other grade levels:* You can adapt the following suggestions to your particular situation. For instance, the explanation provided here for teaching second-grade students about story structure can be used, with slight modification, when teaching the fifth-grade standard *(RL.5.5)* about the overall structure provided by chapters in books, by stanzas in poetry, and by scenes in plays.

PRE-LESSON CONSIDERATIONS

Pre-Instruction Assessment

You will know students are not ready to meet the standard for story structure if, when you ask students to tell you about a story they read, they recite virtually everything that happened rather than using the structure common to all stories to tell just the essential parts.

Large Conceptual Ideas You Can Reinforce during This Lesson

As you teach this lesson, look for opportunities to reinforce big understandings about reading such as the following:

- All well-written text has a structure.
- Using knowledge of a text's structure helps one to comprehend.
- Some information in stories is more important than other information.
- Reading stories can be an engrossing diversion that takes you to different places and different times.

ORGANIZING FOR INSTRUCTION

Embedding Instruction in Reading for Purpose and Understanding

This example is situated in a second-grade classroom where the teacher has as her major goal the instilling of a passion for recreational reading. She provides lots of time for "free reading" during the school day; has students read books of their choice for seat work; ensures that her students are engaged in reading stories of their choice for at least 60 minutes every school day; and encourages book sharing in what she calls "Reader's Chair." The last-named is a variation on the "Author's Chair" idea often used as part of writing instruction, in which a student shares a favorite book in a central location with fellow students gathered around. When observing Reader's Chair, the teacher has noted that some students' retellings drag on too long. She assessed whether they could meet the standard for story structure, and it was clear that they did not meet the standard. So she formed a temporary group of these students who need to meet that standard and uses Eva Bunting's *The Wall* (Clarion Books, 1990) to explain how story structure can be used to summarize.

Ideas for Differentiated Instruction

One idea you could use if you were this teacher: Students not working with you on this standard read books of their choice, consistent with the teacher's vision for developing enthusiastic recreational readers. If they don't have a book to read, they pick a story to read on their iPads.

THE LESSON

Display, Post, or State the Objective

"By the end of this lesson, you will be able to use knowledge about story structure to retell your stories during 'Reader's Chair' more quickly and more efficiently."

Introducing the Lesson

Say something like:

> "You have all enjoyed sharing favorite books during 'Reader's Chair,' but sometimes the sharing takes so long that we run out of time and other students don't get a chance to share. So today I'm going to show you a strategy you can use to share your books more quickly. Instead of telling everything that happened in the story, you will be able to retell just the most important parts of the story."

Stating the Secret to Doing It

Say something like:

> "To do this, you must first understand that all stories have a structure in which the important things happen in a certain sequence. So if we know what that structure is and keep it in mind as we retell our stories, we can retell a story without telling every single thing that happened."

Modeling the Thinking

Say something like:

> "Let me show you how I do it. I have just finished reading this book called *The Wall* [by Eve Bunting; Clarion Books, 1990]. To get ready

to share it during 'Reader's Chair,' I use a story map. A story map is like a picture of the major parts of a story. By using it when I share my story, I can tell the important things that happened in a story. Here's what a story map looks like:

Beginning
- Where is the story happening?
- Who are the characters?
- What is the problem the characters are facing?

Middle
- What two or three major things happened as the characters tried to solve the problem?

End
- How was the problem solved in the end or how did it end?

"When I am going to share a story in 'Reader's Chair,' I use the map to help me. First, I tell where the story happened, who the main characters were and the problem they were facing in this story. Right here on the first page, I find out that the characters in the story are a boy and his dad. The story is happening at a wall, and using my prior knowledge and the picture clues, I can predict that it is the Vietnam Memorial. And it says the problem is to find Grandfather's name on the wall. So now I have the first part of my retelling. I can start by saying, 'This is a story of a boy and his dad who are looking for Grandfather's name on the Vietnam Memorial.' In just one sentence, I have retold the beginning.

"So then I begin thinking about how to retell the middle of the book. The story map says I should tell just two or three major things that happened. There are lots of things there, but I can't tell everything. So I have to decide what the most important details are. Which two or three things would be most helpful to my audience when I share the story? One thing that seems important is that lots of other people are there too. Another thing that seems important is that when they find Grandfather's name they rub a pencil lead sideways over a sheet of paper so that the name shows. And a third thing that seems important is that Dad stands at the wall for a long time, even after others have left. So during Reader's Chair I can tell those important middle parts of the story.

"Then I have to think about how to end my retelling. How was the problem solved at the end? They did find Grandfather's name on the wall, and they put a picture of the boy by the wall. But the story ends with the boy thinking that he would rather have his grandfather with him.

"So if I put the beginning together with the two or three important things in the middle and with the way the problem was solved at the end, I have a brief retelling of my story. We call that a summary. When we share our stories in Reader's Chair, we should use the parts of the story map to help us create a brief retelling."

Scaffolded Assistance

Level 1: Extensive Teacher Help

Say something like:

"So let's try it again, but this time I will do it with Sarah and a book she has just finished reading. So, Sarah, let's use the story map to guide our thinking as we decide how to retell your story. Let's look at the beginning. Here are the two main characters, and here is where it's happening. So what is the problem? Okay, those are the things to retell first. Now we have to look at the middle and figure out what two or three major things would be most important to include in our retelling. You decide what is most important to include by pretending that you are the one listening to the retelling—what would be most helpful to you if you were listening to this retelling? Okay, once we've decided that, we need to think what to report as the ending. How was the problem in the story solved? When we put those beginning, middle, and ending parts together, we have a summary—a brief retelling for our Reader's Chair sharing."

Level 2: Less Teacher Help

Say something like:

"Now let's try another one. But this time I will provide less help. Rodrigo, let's do your book. We'll use the story map to help us. What do you need to do first? Yes, we need to look at the beginning so we can tell where the story happened, who the characters were and the problem they were having. Then we look at the middle. What two or three things do you think are most important to tell about the middle? And then what? Yes, we look at the end and decide what we should tell about how the story ended. Put those things together and you have a brief summary to use when you do Reader's Chair."

Level 3: No Teacher Help

As the Reader's Chair activity continues, remind students to use the story map to organize their retellings. Provide assistance as needed.

Continued Application to Reading

The application would continue during subsequent "Reader's Chair" occasions. However, the teacher will also look for opportunities to remind students to use their understanding of story structure when they are retelling other narratives such as books the teacher reads to the class orally or movies students have seen.

POST-LESSON CONSIDERATIONS

Post-Instruction Assessment

You will know students are ready to meet the standard for story structure if, when asked to provide, in Reader's Chair or in other situations, a brief summary of a story they've read, they specify a beginning, middle, and end, and can describe how they used story structure to keep the summary brief.

Links to Common Core Writing Standards

Story structure is just as important in learning to write stories as it is in learning to comprehend stories. For instance, one second-grade writing standard reads as follows: *W.2.3: Write narratives in which they use a well-established event or short sequence of events, include details to describe actions, thoughts, feelings, use temporal words to signal event order, and provide a sense of closure.* The "event or short sequence" in stories should follow the common story structure. Consequently, teaching students to use a story map when composing stories is learned best when combined with having students use a story map to interpret stories they are reading.

Example 8

Point of View
(CRAFT AND STRUCTURE—RL STANDARD 6)

Note: Point of view also appears as a standard in Informational Text (see, for instance, RI.3.6). The process described here for distinguishing and using point of view when comprehending literature can be applied also when helping students meet the point of view standard for Informational Text.

BACKGROUND

Literature always has a narrator. Sometimes a story is told "in the first person"—that is, the narrator is one of the characters in the story, and what we learn is that character's point of view; as readers, we know what the character knows. At other times, a story is told "in the third person"—the narrator is a god-like entity who stands above the action, and we learn what all the characters are thinking and doing; as readers, we have a view of everyone in the story. Stories are described differently depending on the narrator's point of view. When readers understand this, they can use the narrator's point of view to help them anticipate meaning.

To teach point of view, the predicting–monitoring–repredicting cycle is key. Once students recognize who is telling a story, they can make predictions about how the story will be told, monitor those predictions, and modify the initial prediction or make new predictions if in subsequent pages the early predictions do not come true. The reader anticipates meaning based on an understanding of who is telling the story.

This example is based on the Common Core standard *RL.5.6*: *Describe how a narrator or speaker's point of view influences how events are described.* Consequently, it assumes a fifth-grade situation.

Note for teachers of other grade levels: You can adapt the suggestions provided here to your situation. For instance, second-grade teachers can use a book such as Cynthia Rylant's *The Old Woman Who Named Things* (Harcourt Brace, 1996) to teach standard *RL.2.6: Acknowledge differences in the points of view of characters, including by speaking in a different voice for each character when reading dialogue aloud.* As in the explanation provided here, the teacher would have students use their predicting–monitoring–repredicting skills to predict how the voices of different characters with different points of view would vary.

PRE-LESSON CONSIDERATIONS

Pre-Instruction Assessment

You will know students are not ready to meet the standard for "point of view" if, during discussions of stories, they cannot answer questions such as, "Through whose eyes is the story being told?" and "How are stories told differently when the narrator is first person as opposed to when the narrator is third person?"

Large Conceptual Ideas You Can Reinforce during This Lesson

As you teach this lesson, look for opportunities to reinforce big understandings about reading such as the following:

- Reading comprehension involves thinking ahead and making predictions about what is to come.
- What authors decide about who should tell the story is a big clue that can be used to predict the meaning to follow.
- Writers of stories decide whether to tell the story in the first person or in the third person because of the way they want story events to occur.

ORGANIZING FOR INSTRUCTION

Embedding Instruction in Reading for Purpose and Understanding

This example assumes a fifth-grade classroom where the teacher has initiated a unit on what makes some literature worthy of awards. As part of the unit, the teacher is reading Newbery Award-winning books, as well as other award-winning books, orally to the class, and is encouraging students to read books they've selected themselves. The ultimate goal is for students to write a review of books they've nominated for awards, specifying the characteristics that make a book worthy of an award. However, the teacher's kid watching has indicated that some students are not using narrator point of view to help them comprehend how the story events will be described. Consequently, "inside" the unit of award-winning books, the teacher plans to teach a lesson on point of view to this small group.

Ideas for Differentiating Instruction

One idea you could use if you were this teacher: Some students not working with you on this standard complete work on long-term contracts the teacher has developed for each student on the basis of students' goals and of the teacher's assessment of what each student needs to work on; other students not working with you begin working on their reviews of award-winning books.

THE LESSON

Display, Post, or State the Objective

"By the end of this lesson, you will be able to identify who is telling the story and will be able to make predictions about how narrator point of view influences how story events are related."

Introducing the Lesson

Say something like:

> "Stories are written by an author, but the author decides how the story should be told. Sometimes the author has a character in the story tell the story. This is called a 'first-person' narrator. Sometimes the narrator is a person who knows what all the characters are thinking. This

is called a 'third-person' narrator. It is important to identify who is telling the story because if you know who's telling the story, you can make better predictions about story meaning. Today, we're going to learn how to use point of view to make predictions about stories. After we get done here, you will then be able to use our knowledge of point of view as part of your reviews of books you think should get awards."

Stating the Secret to Doing It

Say something like:

"The secret to using point of view when you read is to, first, identify who is telling the story, and to then use what you know about first person and third person to predict how story events will be influenced."

Modeling the Thinking

Say something like:

"Let me show you how I use point of view to make predictions about story events. Let's look first at this Newbery Award-winning book [holds up Katherine Applegate's *The One and Only Ivan*; Harper, 2012]. Right away on page 1, it says, 'I am Ivan. I am a gorilla.' So I know this is a story told in first person, because a character in the story is the narrator. So I think to myself, if the gorilla is telling his own story, what can I predict about how things will happen in the story? I know that if it were me telling my own story, I'd tell it from my perspective, not from the perspective of others. So I predict Ivan will be telling only how he feels, not how others feel. So I read on to pages 2 and 3 and see that, indeed, he is talking about himself and what he thinks. He definitely has strong opinions, but we only hear his opinions because he is telling the story.

"Now let's look at another Newbery Award winner [holds up Jean George's *Julie of the Wolves*; HarperCollins, 1972]. Right away on the first page I find out that this is going to be about Miyax. But who is telling the story? I know it is a third-person narrator because, in the fourth line down, it says, 'she put down her cooking pot'; if it was a first-person story, it would have said, 'I put down my cooking pot.' So now that I know it is a third-person point of view, I can predict that I will learn not only about Miyax and what she is thinking but also about other characters and what they are thinking. As

I read along, I find out my prediction was correct because I learn what Miyax is thinking as she tries to get the attention of the wolf, Amaroq, but I also find out what Amaroq is doing and thinking. So events in this story are going to include information about all the characters."

Scaffolded Assistance

Level 1: Extensive Teacher Help

Say something like:

"Now let's look at some other Newbery Award winners and see if we can determine point of view and how that is going to influence story events. First, let's look at *The Evolution of Calpurnia Tate* [by Jacqueline Kelly; Henry Holt and Company, 2009]. Let's look at the first sentence: 'By 1899, we had learned. . . .' Just in that little bit, I can tell point of view. What tells us the point of view? Yes, because the author uses the word *we*, we know this will be a first-person story. And what can we predict about how the story will go if we know that Calpurnia is telling the story? Will we hear what all the characters are thinking? No, so we predict we'll hear Calpurnia's side of events. So let's read on to page 2. What are we finding? Yes, Calpurnia says, 'I was eleven years old and the only girl out of seven children. Can you imagine a worse situation?' She's telling the story from her perspective; we are not likely to learn much about what other people are thinking."

Level 2: Less Teacher Help

Say something like:

"Okay, let's look at another Newbery Award winner. This is one of my all-time favorite books [holds up Walter D. Edmonds's *The Matchlock Gun*; Dodd, Mead & Company, 1941]. Let's see if we can determine point of view and how that will influence story events. Read the first page. Who is telling the story? Is it one of the characters? No, we can tell that the story is going to be about Edward, but he is not telling the story. It's being told by a third person. So if it's a third person, what can we predict about what we'll learn as we read this story? Yes, we'll probably learn what many characters are thinking and doing. So does that prediction come true on the next pages? Yes, we find out what Edward thinks, but we also find out what his mother, Gertrude, thinks. So knowing point of view has helped us make accurate predictions about story events.

Level 3: No Teacher Help

Okay, now let's see if you can determine point of view on your own and make your own predictions about how story events will be influenced. Let's use this Newbery Award winner [holds up Scott O'Dell's *Island of the Blue Dolphins*; Houghton Mifflin, 1960]. Who's telling this story? Yes, the very first word on page 1 is *I*, so we know it is a first-person story. So what are you predicting because of that? Yes, we are going to hear story events from the perspective of the Indian girl because she's the one telling the story.

Continued Application to Reading

As students continue to read, listen to, and discuss award-winning books, they will apply what they have learned about point of view and how it can be used to predict how story events will be influenced. Further, as they move on to other units and read other literature, they will continue to use point of view to aid their comprehension.

POST-LESSON CONSIDERATIONS

Post-Instruction Assessment

You will know students are ready to meet the standard for "point of view" if, during discussions of books, students can answer questions about a story's point of view and how it influenced the events in the story.

Links to Common Core Writing Standards

The Common Core specifies for fifth grade that students should be writing narratives and, specifically, that they should be establishing a narrator (see W.5.3a: *Orient the reader by establishing a situation and introducing a narrator. . . .*). Student use of point of view in writing will be strengthened if it is integrated with what they learn about point of view in reading.

Example 9

Illustrations and Text Meaning

(INTEGRATION OF KNOWLEDGE AND IDEAS—
RL STANDARD 7)

BACKGROUND

Visual elements, as well as words, carry meaning. Readers are aided in comprehending literature if they integrate the meaning of visual elements with the meaning of the words in the text. Visual elements begin with illustrations in the lower grades and culminate in upper grades with multimedia elements such as film, video, and staged presentations.

> To teach how to integrate illustrations and text, you begin by establishing that illustrations carry meaning and that they should be used when comprehending text meaning. With those understandings as a basis, readers then use their background knowledge about what is seen in the illustration to predict meanings that may not be explicitly stated in words. Consequently, the predicting–monitoring–repredicting cycle is a prerequisite.

The example provided here focuses on integrating illustrations with textual meaning. It is based on the Common Core standard *RL.3.7*: *Explain how specific aspects of a text's illustrations contribute to what is conveyed by the words in a story (e.g., create mood, emphasize aspects of a character or setting)*. It assumes a hypothetical third-grade classroom.

> *Note for teachers of other grade levels:* The following suggestions can be adapted to your situation. For instance, the process described here for third grade in which students use their background knowledge and predicting is

114

the same as the process fifth graders employ for *RL.7.5: Analyze how visual and multimedia elements contribute to the meaning, tone, or beauty of a text (e.g., graphic novel, multimedia presentation of fiction, folktale, myth, poem).*

PRE-LESSON CONSIDERATIONS

Pre-Instruction Assessment

You will know students are not ready to meet the standard for "illustrations and text meaning" if, during discussions of stories and poems, students are unable to answer questions such as, "When you look at this illustration, what do you think the author wants you to feel?" or "What does this illustration tell you about the character?"

Large Conceptual Ideas You Can Reinforce during This Lesson

As you teach this lesson, look for opportunities to reinforce big understandings about reading such as the following:

- Illustrations convey meaning just as words convey meaning.
- Comprehension always involves using your background experience to make predictions about what the meaning might be, and then confirming or rejecting that prediction in subsequent pages of the text.
- Illustrations not only carry meaning but the art in the illustrations can be enriching—the beauty can stir our emotions.

ORGANIZING FOR INSTRUCTION

Embedding Instruction in Reading for Purpose and Understanding

This example assumes a third-grade class in which students are engaged in writing their own stories for submission to a regional "Writing Rally." To help her students understand the power of stories generally (and, potentially, the power of their own stories), the teacher wants to share with the class William Joyce's *The Fantastic Flying Books of Mr. Morris Lessmore* (Atheneum Books, 2012), a lushly illustrated book. However, having previously noted that some students did not meet the standard regarding using illustrations to help them comprehend text, the teacher first groups those students together to teach a lesson on how to integrate illustrations and text meaning. They will then apply that learning when she later reads *The Fantastic Flying Books of Mr. Morris Lessmore* with the whole class.

Ideas for Differentiating Instruction

One idea you could use if you were this teacher: Students not working with you on this standard work with a partner on writing the stories they are preparing for submission to the Writing Rally, using as a guide a rubric describing the criteria judges will use to rate submissions.

THE LESSON

Display, Post, or State the Objective

"By the end of this lesson, you will be able to use illustrations to extend the meaning of the words in text."

Introducing the Lesson

Say something like:

> "You are all writing your own stories for submission to the regional Writing Rally. So I want to share this book with the whole class [holds up *The Fantastic Flying Books of Mr. Morris Lessmore*] because it is a wonderful story about the power of stories. But because this is an illustrated book in which much of the meaning is conveyed through the illustrations, I want to first show this small group how to use the illustrations in a book or in poetry to increase your comprehension of the text when we read it to the whole class.

Stating the Secret to Doing It

Say something like:

> "To use illustrations to help you comprehend, you first must understand that illustrations convey meaning just as words do. So when you look at an illustration, you use what you know about what you

see in the illustration to make a prediction about what the meaning is. Then you use your predicting–monitoring–repredicting skills to see if that prediction holds up as you read on."

Modeling the Thinking

Say something like:

"Let me show you how I do it, and then you can try to do what I do. Let's start with easier picture books. We can start with this book of poetry by Sylvia Plath [goes to *www.brainpickings.org*, brings up Plath's *The Bed Book*, illustrated by Quentin Blake (Faber Children's Books, 1976), and displays it on her white board/smart board]. Because I know that illustrations convey meaning, I am already expecting to get meaning when I look at the pen-and-ink illustrations on the cover of this book. I look at the pictures of the kids on the cover and see that they are all smiling. I know from my own experience that if they are smiling, this book about beds will be about fun things. I can make that prediction just from looking at the pictures. As I read the poems in the book, I will monitor that prediction to see if it is correct.

"Let's try another example. Let's use this Caldecott Award-winning book [holds up Kevin Henkes's *Kitten's First Full Moon*; Greenwillow Books, 2004]. It's another easy book that you may have read before, but I can use it to show you how I use illustrations to get more meaning. On the first two pages, Kitten thinks she sees a bowl of milk in the sky and tries to drink it. But look at the picture on page 3. When I look at that picture of Kitten, I think to myself, 'What does Kitten's face in that picture make me think she is feeling?' Yes, her eyes look puzzled to me, so I'm going to predict that Kitten can't figure out what's happening. But when I turn the page, I see another picture of Kitten. Her eyes look different to me in this illustration. It looks to me like she's thinking. It doesn't say that in the words, but I can infer that from the picture. So I make the prediction that she is still going to keep trying to get what she thinks is a bowl of milk.

"See how I am expecting to get meaning from the illustrations, and how I'm using my knowledge about what I see in the pictures to predict meaning that may not be conveyed by the words?"

Scaffolded Assistance

Level 1: Extensive Teacher Help

Say something like:

> "Okay, now let's see if we can do one together. Here's another Calde-cott Award-winning book [holds up Molly Bang's *When Sophie Gets Angry – Really, Really Angry.* . . . ; The Blue Sky Press, 1999]. When we look on page 1, Sophie has a smile on her face. But what do you see on her face on page 2? Yes, her mouth is turned down. Use your own experience. What does it usually mean when someone looks like Sophie looks here? Yes, we can predict that she is angry, even though the words do not say she's angry. So let's read on through pages 3 and 4 and look at the picture of Sophie on page 5. On this page, the words say Sophie is angry. What meaning do you get from the picture? Does your experience confirm what the words say?"

Level 2: Less Teacher Help

Say something like:

> "Let's continue to use the book about Sophie, but now you must do more of the thinking yourselves. As we read through the book, we find out that Sophie goes off by herself, and climbs a tree. Then we see her walking through the woods. The words on the page say, ' . . . and heads for home.' So the words tell us where she is going. But the picture also gives us meaning. How does Sophie look here? In your experience, what do you think the picture is saying about how Sophie is feeling? Yes, she looks content. How did you figure that out? Yes, you used the picture and your own background knowledge to predict how she was feeling even though the words on the page don't say anything about how she was feeling."

Level 3: No Teacher Help

At this point, the teacher could show one of the Fancy Nancy books (for instance, *Fancy Nancy and the Fabulous Fashion Boutique,* by Jane O'Connor; Harper, 2010). Students should be using the illustrations to describe meaning beyond what is written in the text.

Continued Application to Reading

The immediate application of this lesson will occur when the teacher shares with the class *The Fantastic Flying Books of Mr. Morris Lessmore.* Subsequently, the teacher will remind students to apply what they know about integrating illustrations and text in other books they read.

POST-LESSON CONSIDERATIONS

Post-Instruction Assessment

Following instruction, you will know students are ready to meet the standard for illustrations and text meaning if they can describe how illustrations provide meaning beyond what was provided by the words in the text.

Links to Common Core Writing Standards

The Common Core specifies that third graders should be engaged in writing stories (*W.3.3: Write narrative to develop real or imagined experiences or events using effective technique, descriptive details, and clear event sequences.*) If students are also encouraged to illustrate their stories, they can use what they learned in reading about illustrations conveying feelings or meaning to supplement and enhance with illustrations what they have written.

Example 10

Compare–Contrast

(INTEGRATION OF KNOWLEDGE AND IDEAS— RL STANDARD 9)

BACKGROUND

Comparing and contrasting is fundamental to comprehending literature. Questions such as, "How are these two stories alike, and how are they different?" are common, as are probes such as, "Describe how the theme in this story is the same as or different from the theme in a poem we read."

> To teach compare–contrast, students should already know how to question as they read, and how to use text clues and their background knowledge to determine what meaning the author is implying. The ability to employ the predict–monitor–repredict cycle is also fundamental. Once the meanings of what are being compared or contrasted are determined, those meanings must be set side by side to determine how they are the same or different.

The example provided here is based on the grade 6 Common Core standard *RL.6.9: Compare and contrast texts in different forms or genres (e.g., stories and poems; historical novels and fantasy stories) in terms of their approaches to similar themes and topics.* It assumes a hypothetical sixth-grade classroom.

> *Note to teachers of other grade levels:* You can adapt the teaching suggestions provided here to your particular situation. For instance, first graders working on *RL1.9: With prompting and support, compare and contrast the*

adventures and experiences of characters in familiar stories would use the same process of determining the meanings of the two stories (such as familiar fairy tales) and then setting the two different adventures side by side for purposes of compare and contrast.

PRE-LESSON CONSIDERATIONS

Pre-Instruction Assessment

You will know students are not ready to meet the standard for "compare and contrast" if they are unable to provide answers when asked questions such as, "How is this story the same or different from the story we read yesterday?" or "How was this character's actions different from another character's actions?"

Large Conceptual Ideas You Can Reinforce during This Lesson

As you teach this lesson, look for opportunities to reinforce big understandings about reading such as the following:

- The best literature is more than just an interesting story or poem; it almost always has a message or "big idea" about life and living.
- Authors of literature almost always have a "big conclusion" they want you to understand, but they usually imply it rather than state it explicitly.
- In order to determine implied meaning, readers must be assertive *creators* of meaning; but that meaning must be consistent with what is stated in the text.
- Literature often conveys important messages about life and how to live it well.

ORGANIZING FOR INSTRUCTION

Embedding Instruction in Reading for Purpose and Understanding

This example is set in a middle school in which an advanced sixth-grade class is reading literature selections as part of a project in which the goal is to develop understandings about the role fate plays in the human condition. Yesterday, the students read two poems—Robert Frost's "The Road Not Taken" and William Butler Yeats's "An Irish Airman Foresees

His Death"—and then discussed the meaning of Yeats's poem. Because a small group of students have not yet met the standard for compare–contrast, the teacher returns to the two poems the next day and teaches compare–contrast to this group.

Ideas for Differentiating Instruction

One idea you could use if you were this teacher: Students not working with you on this standard use computers and/or iPads to do Internet research on other poems that can be used to understand the role fate plays in the human condition.

THE LESSON

Display, Post, or State the Objective

"By the end of this lesson, you will be able to describe the meaning of two poems and compare them to determine whether the authors' conclusions in the two poems are the same or different."

Lesson Introduction

Say something like:

> "Yesterday, we read and talked about both "The Road Not Taken" and "An Irish Airman Foresees His Death." We looked particularly closely at Yeats's poem about the airman. We decided that, in terms of our project on what influences human life, Yeats seems to be saying that humans are controlled by fate. Now we want to look at Frost's poem and compare what he's saying about human life with what Yeats is saying. We want to decide whether the two authors are conveying the same meaning or a different meaning."

Stating the Secret to Doing It

Say something like:

> "In order to compare and contrast our two poems (or two stories or two of anything), we first have to use our predicting–monitoring–

repredicting skills to determine the meaning Robert Frost is conveying in his poem. Then we have to set Frost's meaning side by side with Yeats's meaning and examine them to decide whether they are saying the same thing or different things."

Modeling the Thinking

Say something like:

> "As readers, we know that authors are trying to get us to think in certain ways without actually stating it directly. And we already know from our discussion yesterday that Yeats seems to be saying that life is controlled by fate. Now we have to look at what Frost is saying and compare it with what Yeats is saying.
>
> "We have already decided that Frost is using the road as a metaphor for life and that the fork in the road is a life choice. But what is he saying about that choice? Let's look at what he says when encountering two alternative ways in the path:

> > Oh, I kept the first for another day!
> > Yet knowing how way leads on to way,
> > I doubted if I should ever come back.

> "I know the poem is about life and that the fork in the road is a choice in life. But what is Frost saying about what influences human life? To answer that, I have to look at the words and use my own experience to make a prediction and monitor whether that meaning holds up in future lines in the poem. When he says he kept one fork for another day, my experience tells me he plans to travel down the other path at some later time. But then he says he doubts that he will ever come back. So I have to predict here what it is Frost is trying to get me to conclude. To figure out what he is telling me, I think about my own experience. Have I ever said I would do something and really meant to return to do it but then failed to get around to it? If that is my experience, I predict that Frost is saying the same thing about choices in life. So I think he wants me to conclude that life is a matter of humans making choices. So let's read on, monitor that prediction, and see if it remains unchanged."

Scaffolded Assistance

Level 1: Extensive Teacher Help

Say something like:

> "Now let's look at another example, but this time you help me do the thinking. Let's look at the first two lines in the last stanza. Frost says:
>
> > I shall be telling this with a sigh
> > Somewhere ages and ages hence:
>
> "So what does Frost mean here? We know he's talking about life choices. Let's look at the clues he provides. He says he will be talking about his choice 'with a sigh.' So how do you figure out what he means here? Yes, you use your own experience. How do you feel when you do something 'with a sigh'? Okay, some of you say it means you are sad; some of you say you have regrets. So saying it 'with a sigh' means being sad about it or having regrets about it. So what do you suppose Frost means when he says this? Yes, he too is probably sad or regretful that he couldn't take both roads. Now let's think about what he's saying regarding our questions about what influences human life. Can we still say he seems to mean that humans make choices? Yes. So now set that side by side with what we said Yeats seems to be saying about what influences human life. Yeats says it is fate; Frost says it is human choice. Are they saying the same thing or different things about what influences human life?"

Level 2: Less Teacher Help

Say something like:

> "Now let's look at the last two lines on the poem. What do we need to do first? Yes, we have to use clues in the poem and our own prior experience to figure out the meaning he is conveying. So what clues are there? Yes, he says you should take the road few people take— the 'road less traveled.' Is he still saying humans make choices?"

Level 3: No Teacher Help

Students can list what Frost seems to be saying about what influences human life, then list what Yeats seems to be saying, and then compare the two. Are they saying the same thing? Or are they saying something different?

Continued Application to Reading

In this particular sixth-grade situation, application will occur as the teacher and students continue to pursue in other literature the question about what influences human life. Other selections will be read, other conclusions will be drawn, and students will continue to compare and contrast the meanings conveyed by different authors.

POST-LESSON CONSIDERATIONS

Post-Instruction Assessment

You will know students are ready to meet the standard for compare and contrast if you observe students using their prior knowledge to decide what authors want the reader to think, and then setting it side by side with what other authors are saying and decide whether they are saying the same thing or different things.

Links to Common Core Writing Standards

Compare–contrast requires two or more things to be compared and is most directly associated with reading rather than writing. However, when young writers learn to construct narratives, they must be conscious of being clear enough for their stories to be compared with other stories, This goal is implicit in the Common Core writing standard *W.6.3b: Use narrative techniques such as dialogue, pacing, and description to develop experiences, events, and/or characters.* Teaching this writing standard in conjunction with compare–contrast in reading often helps students become more proficient in both reading and writing.

EXAMPLES FOR EXPLAINING
INFORMATIONAL TEXT

Example 11

Main Idea

(KEY IDEAS AND DETAILS—RI STANDARD 2)

Note: This section begins with Standard 2 in Informational Text because Standard 1 is "Reading for Details," and you can use Example 1 in the Literature section when teaching "Reading for Details" in Informational Text.

BACKGROUND

Main idea refers to the most important idea found in informational text. That is, when all the details are considered together, what is the author's main message? Literature also has "a most important idea" or "main message," but we call it "theme" (see Example 3).

Main idea is more than just the topic. In a book about locomotives, for instance, the topic may be "locomotives," but the main idea is what the author wants readers to understand is important about locomotives.

Main idea is difficult to teach for three reasons. First, while a main idea is sometimes stated in a topic sentence in the introductory paragraph, most of the time the main idea is implied rather than stated explicitly. Second, to determine main idea, the reader must look across several pages of text, note a variety of details, and, by tying the details together, predict what the main idea is. Third, the predictions we make for main idea are tentative—we must be ready to change our prediction as we encounter new information.

To teach main idea, first establish the understanding that authors write informational text because they have something important to say (i.e., a main idea). Second, have readers use background knowledge about clues in the text (the details and what links the details together) to make a prediction about what the main idea is, monitor that prediction, and make a new prediction about the main idea when new details are encountered.

The following example is based on Common Core standard *RI.3.2: Determine the main idea of a text; recount the key details and explain how they support the main idea.* The example assumes a hypothetical third-grade classroom.

Note for teachers of other grade levels: The thinking process described for this third grade can be adapted and used to teach main idea thinking in different informational text and at different grade levels. For instance, seventh graders studying Australia and faced with standard *RI.7.2: Determine two or more central ideas in a text and analyze their development over the course of the text . . .* might use the book *Unique Animals and Birds of Australia* by Michael Morcombe (Lansdowne Press, 1973). While the text will be more complex, identifying central ideas is still a process of combining details together in much the same way as described for third grade.

PRE-LESSON CONSIDERATIONS

Pre-Instruction Assessment

You will know students are not ready to meet the standard for main idea if, when students read informational text, they cannot correctly answer questions about what the author's main message is or what the most important idea is.

Large Conceptual Ideas You Can Reinforce during This Lesson

As you teach this lesson, look for opportunities to reinforce big understandings about reading such as the following:

- Authors of informational text write because they feel strongly about the topic.
- Topic and main idea are not the same.

- Key details are important to note, but combining them to determine the author's main idea is more important.
- Not every word or detail is important in determining main idea.
- Determining main idea requires aggressive questioning and thinking as one reads.

ORGANIZING FOR INSTRUCTION

Embedding Instruction in Reading for Purpose and Understanding

This example is set in a third grade. It assumes a class that has been studying flowers in science. Because the teacher wants her students to read for purpose and understanding, she has approached the study of flowers from the perspective of what third graders can do to promote preservation of wild flowers. Yesterday, the teacher introduced the informational text *Meadow: A Close-Up Look at the Natural World of a Meadow*, by Barbara Taylor (Dorling Kindersley, 1992), and she and the class discussed how they might use the information to preserve flowers in nature. Today, the teacher forms a small group of students who have not met the standard for main idea and returns to the book, using it as an opportunity to teach students how to determine main idea in informational text.

Ideas for Differentiating Instruction

One idea you could use if you were this teacher: Students who are not working with you on this standard complete previously prepared tiered assignments in which they use an accompanying study guide to read text about how third graders could preserve wild flowers.

THE LESSON

Post, Display, or State the Objective

"By the end of this lesson, you will be able to state what the author is saying is the most important message in the text, and you will be able to describe the thinking you did to decide what was most important."

Introducing the Lesson

Say something like:

"Yesterday we began reading this book on meadows, and we discussed how we might use the information to decide how to preserve wild flowers in nature. Today we're going to return to this book so I can show you how to determine what the author is saying is the most important idea in the text. We call this the 'main idea.' It's hard to do because authors seldom come right out and tell us the main idea; instead, they give us details and expect us to use those details as clues to figure it out for ourselves. Let me show you how I try to figure out main idea, and then we will try some together. We will then use the author's main idea to help us learn how to preserve flowers in nature."

The Secret to Doing It

Say something like:

"To figure out what a main idea is, you must put yourself in the author's place, because authors of informational text usually have something important they want to communicate. So you need to keep that in mind and then use the details the author provides, and the way those ideas seem to go together, to make a prediction about what the most important idea is. As you encounter more details, you must monitor to see if your prediction is still making sense and, if it's not, you need to make a new prediction."

Modeling the Thinking

Say something like:

"Let me show you how I do it. Look first in Chapter 1 and follow along in your own copy. We read it yesterday, but now we are going to return to the text to see what the author wants us to understand is most important. To decide that, I must first get inside the author's head—I know authors write because they have something important to tell us, so I begin with that idea. The author, Barbara Taylor, gives me details about the meadow, and I can use them as clues.

On page 8, for instance, she provides details such as the meadow is 'full of colorful flowers' and is 'buzzing with insects' and is 'home to many animals' [lists these phrases on the board and links them together]. These are all clues. So I stop and reflect on those. I say to myself, 'What does my own experience suggest to me about how these details go together—about what they all have in common.' In my experience, all those details seem to be about pleasant things. Maybe the author's big idea at this point is that meadows are pleasant places, so I make a prediction that this is the main idea. I can't be sure that's the right main idea; I may have to change it later. So I read on, keeping that prediction in mind. But when I read the next two sentences, that main idea no longer seems to make sense. The details the author states here say that meadows 'have been plowed over' and that 'wildlife finds it hard to survive' [highlights these and links them]. So I stop and think again: 'What do these details all have in common? What could be the big idea here?' When I combine those ideas in my mind, it doesn't sound like things are pleasant. So I think I will have to repredict. Why does the author provide those details? What is she trying to get me to think? In my experience, it doesn't sound like it is a good thing for the meadow. So I make a new prediction—that the most important thing the author is trying to tell me is that the good things in meadows are lost if we plow them over.

"So to figure out the main idea, I have to stop reading sometimes and ask myself questions such as, 'Why are these details here? What does my experience suggest the big idea might be when you look at these details in combination?' Can you see that you have to be thoughtful and use a lot of energy in questioning why the author is saying what she is saying?"

Scaffolded Assistance

Level 1: Extensive Teacher Help

Say something like:

"Let's now try doing this together. Let's look at Chapter 3, which we read yesterday, but now we want to use it to figure out the main idea. The chapter is titled 'Flower Power.' The title is a detail we can use to make a prediction about what the author thinks is most important. What does your experience make you think when you see the words *flower power*? Yes, we've heard phrases like this before, and it usually means that something is powerful. So we make a prediction that the author wants us to think flowers are powerful. So let's read on, and let's see if that prediction holds up. Now we read that wild flowers are 'attractive' and provide 'food and shelter for many creatures.' These are details. It's sometimes hard to keep all this in your mind, so let's look at them separately and link them so we can stop and think about them [lists them on the board]. As we look at them, let's think together about how we could combine them. What does our experience make us think is important here? Yes, it seems the author wants us to think that wild flowers are important. Is that different from our first prediction that flowers are powerful? No, so we don't have to repredict. At this point, it seems that the main idea is that flowers are important.

"Can you see how the thinking you did helped us figure out the main idea? You found details, combined them together, and used your experience to figure out what the common idea was across the details. We can predict that the common idea across the details is the main idea."

Level 2: Less Teacher Help

Say something like:

"Let's see if you can figure out the main idea if you do more of the work and we don't display the details on the smart board. Look at the section on page 13 called 'Late Developers.' What are we going to do to figure out the main idea here? Yes, we're going to look at the details the author provides, and we're going to use our experience to figure out what the details in combination make us think. So what are the details? Yes, one detail is that insects spread the pollen for the flowers; another is that flowers provide food for insects. You can write those details down if it makes it easier to think about them. So what do you think these details mean when combined? Yes, it seems that insects do good things for flowers and flowers do good things for insects. So are you thinking of what the author wants us to think is important? Yes, good. The author seems to want us to think that insects and flowers depend on each other. So that is probably the main idea in that section."

Level 3: No Teacher Help

Students read subsequent sections of the book on meadows independently, reporting on what they think the main idea is and describing how they used details and their own background knowledge to figure it out.

Continued Application to Reading

In pursuing their project on how to preserve wild flowers, students will be reading other books on flowers. Students should be reminded to look for the author's most important idea in those informational texts, as well as in other content areas such as social studies.

POST-LESSON CONSIDERATIONS

Post-Instruction Assessment

You will know students are ready to meet the standard for main idea if, after reading an informational text, students can state what the author's most important message was and can describe how they used the details to decide it.

Links to Common Core Writing Standards

Main idea is as important in composing informational text as it is in comprehending informational text. To be a good writer, one must be able to compose coherent and cohesive text messages in which the details keep the reader "on track" and make clear what the most important idea is. The Common Core reinforces this in its writing standards. For instance, the third-grade writing standard is *W.3.2b: Develop the topic with facts, definitions, and details.* To "develop the topic," a writer must use facts, definitions, and details in a coherent way to make clear what the important message is. Because of the similarities in focus, both the reading and the writing standards for main idea are best developed when taught together.

Example 12

Making Connections and Establishing Relationships
(KEY IDEAS AND DETAILS—RI STANDARD 3)

BACKGROUND

Good readers look for connections and relationships among characters, events, ideas, and different sources of information. In the Common Core standards, the focus is on relationships in historical, scientific, or technical text, with complexity ranging from describing the connection between two individuals or events in kindergarten to analyzing how ideas influence individuals or how individuals influence events in seventh grade. As with much of comprehension, this requires inferential thinking, with students using text clues to make predictions about what conclusion the author wants them to draw from the connections and relationships described in the text.

> To teach students how to make connections and establish relationships, you should first set the expectation that what happens in historical, scientific, and technical text is often the result of interactions among events, individuals, or ideas, and that good readers examine those interactions and draw conclusions about how they influence events. Then readers use their predicting–monitoring–repredicting strategy to search for such interactions as they proceed through text, and question themselves about what conclusion the author expects them to draw about those interactions.

The teaching example provided here is based on the Common Core's fifth-grade standard *RI.5.3: Explain the relationships or interactions between two or more individuals, events, ideas, or concepts in a histori-cal, scientific, or technical text based on specific information in the text.* It assumes a hypothetical fifth-grade classroom.

Note to teachers of other grade levels: The suggestions described here for teaching students to meet the standard for making connections and establishing relationships can be applied to other grade levels. For instance, first-grade teachers, using a big book on Martin Luther King, would use basically the same explanation, establishing the expectation that connections are important and then using a predicting–monitoring–repredicting cycle, to teach standard *RI.1.3: Describe the connection between two individuals, events, ideas, or pieces of information in a text.*

PRE-LESSON CONSIDERATIONS

Pre-Instruction Assessment

You will know students are not ready to meet the standard for making connections and establishing relationships if, when discussing historical, scientific, or technical text, they cannot point to specific sections of the text that describe a relationship or interaction among individuals, events, ideas, or concepts and how it was influential.

Large Conceptual Ideas You Can Reinforce during This Lesson

As you teach this lesson, look for opportunities to reinforce big understandings about reading such as the following:

- Authors often want readers to draw conclusions, even though they may not say so explicitly or do not specify exactly what conclusion should be drawn.
- Connections and relationships must not only be identified but must also be analyzed for how they are important to the text.
- Drawing conclusions about the importance of connections and relationships is a prediction based on your experience.
- Readers must be assertive in creating meaning when it is not stated explicitly.
- Deep understanding resulting from analyzing text enriches our insights about our world.

ORGANIZING FOR INSTRUCTION

Embedding Instruction in Reading for Purpose and Understanding

In this fifth grade, the social studies curriculum focuses on United States history. For each segment of U.S. history, students have been identifying characters famous for their bravery. They have accumulated a list of such people from previous readings. Now they are studying the western movement and, particularly, the Lewis and Clark expedition. The students become particularly interested in the bravery of Sacagawea, and want to learn more about her. The teacher collects a variety of informational text on Sacagawea for student use, and distributes a study guide to those students who have already met the standard for making connections. Then she forms a temporary group consisting of students who have not yet met the standard. She begins by reading and discussing *I Am Sacagawea* by Grace Norwich (Scholastic, 2012).

Ideas for Differentiating Instruction

One idea you could use if you were this teacher: Students not working with you on this standard are working in pairs with the Sacagawea books the teacher provided and with a study guide she prepared that directs them to specific connections and relationships regarding the Lewis and Clark expedition.

THE LESSON

Display, Post, or State the Objective

"By the end of this lesson, you will be able to point to and use specific sections of text on Sacagawea that describe relationships between her and others on the expedition, and state how those relationships influenced the western movement in the United States."

Introducing the Lesson

Say something like:

"We have been interested in Sacagawea because we know she was brave, so we can add her to our collection of brave Americans who influenced our history. But in what ways did Sacagawea influence our history? To find that out, we need to examine her interactions with other people and with other events, and then draw conclusions from those as to how she influenced history. I'll show you how to do it in this book [holds up *I Am Sacagawea*] and then you can try it in some other books I have gathered about Sacagawea."

Stating the Secret to Doing It

Say something like:

> "The secret to using interactions to draw conclusions about how they influenced events is that we must first understand that during historical events such as the Lewis and Clark expedition interactions between individuals or between individuals and events led to particular outcomes. Then we must use our predicting–monitoring–repredicting skills to identify those interactions and use our own experience to draw conclusions about how those interactions influenced those outcomes."

Modeling the Thinking

Say something like:

> "Okay, in reading *I Am Sacagawea*, I need to be thinking about how events or people influenced the western movement and the Lewis and Clark expedition. I use my predicting skills as I read. On pages 20 and 21, I learn that Sacagawea was a Shoshone and lived in the mountains in the west, but that she was captured by the Hidatsa tribe and moved east into the Great Plains. I begin to think how this event interacts with the Lewis and Clark expedition, and I try to predict how what happened to Sacagawea could influence the Lewis and Clark expedition. As I read on, I find out that Lewis and Clark spent the winter of 1804 with the Hidatsa tribe. So this is where Sacagawea meets Lewis and Clark. This is an interaction between two events—one is Sacagawea getting captured and moving east and another is Lewis and Clark moving west and wintering with the Hidatsa. I begin to think about how the two events are connected and why the connection is important. I put those two events side by side and think, 'How do these influence what happens?' I use my

own experience with events and how they influence each other and predict that it is an important connection because if Sacagawea had not been captured, she would not have met Lewis and Clark."

Scaffolded Assistance

Level 1: Extensive Teacher Help

Say something like:

> "As we read on, we learn that Sacagawea was married to a French trader named Charbonneau who was not a member of the expedition. Let's read further and see if there is a relationship here that was important to the success of the expedition. Be looking for connections between people that might be important for the expedition. What do you see on page 42? Yes, there is an interaction between Lewis and Charbonneau. What was that interaction? Yes, Lewis apparently did not like Charbonneau. But despite that, Charbonneau was hired to accompany the expedition. Why was that important? Yes, even though Lewis didn't like Charbonneau, he took him because then he could also have Sacagawea as a translator. It is a connection between two events that influenced the success of Lewis and Clark."

Level 2: Less Teacher Help

Say something like:

> "On page 59, it says Sacagawea became very sick. This event is connected with other events, such as the expedition's need to move on even though she was sick. List those two events. So what is the connection between those two events? Yes. So now use your experience and your own knowledge to predict how the expedition would have been different if Sacagawea had not recovered from her illness."

Level 3: No Teacher Help

The teacher distributes several other books on Sacagawea to the class—for example, Lise Erdrish's *Sacagawea* (Carolrhoda Books, 2003) and Alana White's *Sacagawea* (Enslow Publishers, 1997)—and has students search for and report on other connections of individuals and events during the Lewis and Clark expedition and how those connections were important.

Continued Application to Reading

These fifth-grade students will continue their study of brave individuals who influenced American history. As they continue this project, the teacher will remind them to be looking, in their future reading of American history, for connections and relationships among individuals, events, and ideas and how they were influential.

POST-LESSON CONSIDERATIONS

Post-Instruction Assessment

You will know students are ready to meet the standard for connections and relationships if they are able, during subsequent discussion of social studies or science content, to cite important connections and relationships and why they were important.

Links to Common Core Writing Standards

The Common Core standard W.5.2 states: *Write informative/explanatory texts to examine a topic and convey ideas and information clearly.* Students will be aided in meeting this writing standard if they are encouraged to include in their writing what they have learned in reading about connections and relationships; that is, in their writing of informational text students should be conscious of making clear the important connections and relationships.

Example 13

Word Meaning

(CRAFT AND STRUCTURE—RI STANDARD 4)

BACKGROUND

Vocabulary includes two kinds of word meanings. One kind of word meaning is a *function word*. Function words are used to signal grammatical functions. Words such as *the, into, from, is,* and *although* are function words because they signal grammatical functions. We use them in our oral and written language, but we cannot describe their meaning except in terms of their function in a sentence. Normally, function words are not taught directly; instead, children learn to use function words in the normal course of learning to speak the language.

A second kind of vocabulary word is a *content word,* and content words often *are* taught directly. Content words are labels for concepts we can picture in our minds. For instance, the words *bicycle* and *tricycle* are labels for concepts we can picture in our minds. We can describe them, draw pictures of them, state the features distinguishing one from another, and use words associated with *bicycle* and *tricycle* correctly in oral and written language.

Word meaning is important in terms of the Common Core emphasis on knowledge building. Knowledge is acquired through learning more and more content words. Whenever we encounter new content (e.g., in social studies, in science, through the Internet), we learn new words, and with new words we build new background knowledge. Because background knowledge is a basis of comprehension, word meaning (i.e., content word meaning) is crucial to reading success.

We learn content words through experience—either through direct experience (i.e., experiencing it in reality, or being able to touch it or see it) or through vicarious experience (i.e., reading about it, or being told about it, or seeing it in a video or in an online presentation, or having a teacher teach it). Having a cat as a pet is a direct experience; reading about a cat is a vicarious experience.

Generally speaking, learning vocabulary words through direct experience is more effective than learning them through vicarious experience. In school, however, it is impractical to provide real experiences for the many content words students need to learn. Consequently, in school most vocabulary words are taught vicariously— that is, teachers directly teach the meaning of content words.

> To teach content word meaning, the key is to focus on the features that distinguish the entity in question. Key features distinguish one concept from another. For instance, "barking" is a feature that distinguishes the concept "dog" from another concept we label "cat."

The example provided here is based on Common Core standard *RI. K.4: Ask and answer questions to help determine or clarify the meaning of words and phrases in a text.* It assumes a hypothetical kindergarten classroom.

> *Note for teachers of other grade levels:* You can teach word meaning at other grade levels by adapting the following suggestions to your particular situation. For instance, a fifth-grade teacher using a textbook such as *World Geography* (Glencoe, 1987) will find numerous technical words students may not know and will employ the same process of noting distinguishing features and using them to identify examples and nonexamples of the concepts when teaching to standard *RI.5.4: Determine the meaning of general academic and domain-specific words and phrases in a text relevant to a grade 5 topic or subject area.*

PRE-LESSON CONSIDERATIONS

Pre-Instruction Assessment

You will know students are not ready to meet the standard for "word meaning" if, in a particular content area such as the one in this example, students cannot point to an appropriate picture of the word or correctly use the content word in a sentence, or use it during a discussion.

Large Conceptual Ideas You Can Reinforce during This Lesson

During this lesson, look for opportunities to reinforce big understandings such as the following:

- The things around us in the world have names or labels.
- In reading, these labels are seen as words we say; in writing, these labels are seen as words we write.
- A word we encounter in school content has features that distinguish it from the meaning of other words.
- The more words we know and use, the more knowledge we have and the smarter we are.

ORGANIZING FOR INSTRUCTION

Embedding Instruction in Reading for Purpose and Understanding

This example assumes a kindergarten class engaged in a math lesson on geometry. The class is going to be making pictures with geometric shapes they will then send home to their parents. In preparation for this activity, the teacher is going to share with the students a big book having examples of basic geometric forms, such as squares, circles, and rectangles (e.g., *Shapes and Signs*, by Tina Thoburn and Seymour Reit; Western Publishing, 1963). While reading the big book, the teacher points out the various geometric shapes and their names. When it becomes apparent that two students cannot use those words in discussion, she directly teaches the meaning of each of the geometric words.

Ideas for Differentiating Instruction

One idea you could use if you were this teacher: In this case, the teacher initially reads the big book to the whole class, then assesses whether all students can now point to and identify the geometric shapes. For the two who cannot, she forms a temporary group and works with them while the rest of the class works on drawing the pictures using geometric forms they are going to send home to their parents.

THE LESSON

Display, Post, or State the Objective

"By the end of this lesson, you will be able to name and describe each of the shapes we saw in the big book we read together today."

Introducing the Lesson

Say something like:

> "Today we read a big book that has lots of different shapes in it. We are going to have to know what those shapes are in order to draw our pictures for our parents. So let me tell you the names of each of the shapes and how I tell one from another."

Stating the Secret to Doing It

Say something like:

> "The secret to naming these shapes is to pay attention to what makes one shape different from the other shapes. That is, what features make one shape look different from another shape?"

Modeling the Thinking

Say something like:

> "I have a bunch of wooden shapes here in front of me. Let's start with this one [picks up a square]. This one is called a 'square.' I can always tell a square because it has four corners, and all the sides are equal. When I see a shape with four corners and all sides equal, I know it is called a 'square.' Here, touch this wooden square. Feel the corners.
>
> "Now let's look at this one [picks up a circle]. This one is called a 'circle.' I can always tell a circle because it has no corners; it is all round. When I see a shape like this, I know it is called a 'circle.' Feel this wooded circle. See how it has no corners?
>
> "So let's look at some examples. I'm going to draw two shapes on the board [draws a large square and a small circle]. I know this is

a square [pointing to the square] because it has four corners and all sides are equal. I know this one [pointing to the circle] is an example of a circle because it is round all around and has no corners."

Scaffolded Assistance

Level 1: Extensive Teacher Help

Say something like:

> "Let's look together at this wooden shape [picks up a wooden triangle] and what it has that makes it different from the square and the circle. How many corners does this shape have? Does it have four corners like a square? No, it has three corners, so it can't be a square. This is called a 'triangle.' We can always tell a triangle because it has three corners. Feel the shape of this wooden triangle."

Level 2: Less Teacher Help

Say something like:

> "Here's another shape. Let's examine this shape. Is it different from a square? A circle? A triangle? Why can't it be a square? Yes, even though it has four corners, the sides are not equal. The name of this shape is 'rectangle.' We know it is a rectangle and not a circle because it has corners. It can't be a triangle because it has four corners, not three. It could be a square, but why can't it be a square? Right, the sides are not all equal."

Level 3: No Teacher Help

At the third level of assistance, the teacher may simply name a shape and have students describe the features that make it different from other shapes. For instance, she might say something like:

> "This shape I'm holding is called an oval. What do you see that makes it different from a square or a circle or a triangle or a rectangle?"

Continued Application to Reading

An immediate application of the word meanings will occur when the students use the shapes to draw pictures for their parents. The teacher will then present different books on other days that require naming and describing basic geometric forms.

POST-LESSON CONSIDERATIONS

Post-Instruction Assessment

You will know students are ready to meet the standard for "word meaning" if, during discussion of informational text, students are able to use the new word or words correctly in oral discussions and/or can point to a picture of the word.

Links to Common Core Writing Standards

The Common Core specifies for kindergarten the following writing standard: *W.K.2: Use a combination of drawing, dictating, and writing to compose informative/explanatory texts in which they name what they are writing about and supply some information about the topic.* "Naming what they are writing" is an application of word meaning. Applying in writing a word meaning used in reading makes it more likely that the word meaning will be retained. In the case of this lesson, for instance, a writing task such as drawing a picture for their parents using the geometric shapes will strengthen their learning of these new content words.

Example 14

Using Context Clues to Determine Word Meaning

(CRAFT AND STRUCTURE—RI STANDARD 4)

BACKGROUND

Teachers directly teach many content words, as illustrated in Example 13. However, the Common Core also specifies that students should be able to determine the meaning of words "in a text relevant to the grade level." The major way to learn new words "in a text" is through use of context. Students' vocabulary will expand greatly if they learn to use context clues to figure out the meaning of new words in a text. Using context provides an avenue to independent learning of new vocabulary and is an efficient way to learn new word meanings.

Context is a problem-solving strategy students employ as they are reading text. This example is based on Common Core standard *RI.2.4: Determine the meaning of words and phrases in a text relevant to a grade 2 topic or subject area.* When a new word is encountered in a text, students can use the clues embedded around the new word to figure out for themselves what the word means. Context clues range from fairly straightforward clues, such as direct definition clues, to more subtle clues, such as mood clues. First and second graders can learn to use the more obvious clues through listening activities; upper-grade students can learn to use the more subtle clues in their reading of content material in social studies and science.

To teach how to figure out word meaning using context clues, students must already know how to employ predicting–monitoring–repredicting skills. That is, they look for clues around the unknown word, use those clues and their background knowledge to predict what the word might mean, and then monitor and repredict based on subsequent clues in the text.

This example is situated in a hypothetical second grade and illustrates how in a listening situation students can use context clues to figure out word meaning.

Note to teachers of other grade levels: For teaching this standard in reading (rather than listening) and at other grade levels, adapt the following suggestions to your situation. For instance, the same process of using clues and background experience to predict word meaning can be used when teaching seventh graders to meet standard *RI.7.4: Determine the meaning of words and phrases as they are used in a text, including figurative, connotative, and technical meanings. . . .*

PRE-LESSON CONSIDERATIONS

Pre-Instruction Assessment

You will know students are not ready to meet the standard for using context clues to figure out word meaning if you observe students who cannot tell what a word means even though there are clues to its meaning embedded in the text.

Large Conceptual Ideas You Can Reinforce during This Lesson

As you teach this lesson, look for opportunities to reinforce big understandings about reading such as the following:

- Learning new vocabulary is a key to knowledge building generally and to building knowledge about content areas such as social studies, science, and math.
- New words are opportunities to build knowledge.
- Stopping when reading is a strategy all good readers use when they get "stuck" on a problem such as an unknown word meaning.
- Many words have several meanings, and we use context to decide which meaning is appropriate in that particular sentence.

ORGANIZING FOR INSTRUCTION

Embedding Instruction in Reading for Purpose and Understanding

This example assumes a second-grade class involved in creating a school manual for what to do in severe weather, based on a science unit on weather. Some of the students in the class are reading about various weather phenomena independently. However, the teacher has noted that four mainstreamed special education students cannot use text clues to figure out word meaning, so she groups them together to teach them how to use context. This group is going to read together the book *Tornadoes*, by Seymour Simon (HarperCollins, 1999). The main purpose is to gather information about tornadoes for contribution to the manual the class is producing, but the teacher also uses the occasion to teach context clues.

Ideas for Differentiating Instruction

One idea you could use if you were this teacher: Students not working with you on this standard continue to gather information about weather phenomena independently, using iPads, computers, and books from the library; they follow an outline the teacher provides listing specific information needed for the school manual.

THE LESSON

Display, Post, or State the Objective

"By the end of this lesson, you will have information about tornadoes to tell the rest of the class, but you will also be able to figure out the meaning of difficult words in the book *Tornadoes*, and you will be able to describe how you figured out the meaning of those words."

Introducing the Lesson

Say something like:

"I am going to read to you this book on tornadoes because it will give us information we can contribute to our manual on severe weather. But before we start, I want to show you how to use clues in the text to figure out the meaning of some of the hard words you will hear when you listen to this book. The best way to figure out the meaning of hard words while you're listening or reading is to use the other words around the unknown words as clues. We call this 'using context clues.'"

Stating the Secret to Doing It

Say something like:

> "When you hear a word you don't know, the secret to using context clues to figure out its meaning is to listen for other words that give you clues, then use your background knowledge about those clues to predict what the word might mean, and to then read on and see if that prediction comes true."

Modeling the Thinking

Say something like:

> "I'm going to use some sentences I made up to show you how I use context clues to figure out the meaning of unknown words. Pay attention to how I think my way through the problem because later I'm going to ask you to figure out some hard words using the same kind of thinking. I'll read this sentence as an example [posts the following on chart paper]:
>
> > The buoy floating in the harbor lit the water and warned the ship to stay away from the rocks.
>
> "I have never heard of *buoy* before [circles it on the chart paper]. I don't know what it means. So I stop. I'm going to think about clues that might help me. I heard the word *floating*—that's a clue. And *harbor* is a clue. And *lit* is a clue. And it says the buoy *warned the ship*, so that's a clue too [underlines each clue on the chart paper]. I know from my own experience what a harbor is, and I know what floating is, so a buoy must be something that floats in a harbor. And then it says it is lit, so a buoy must be a light. And then it says it warned the ship away from the rocks and I know from my own experience that you don't want to hit rocks when you are in a boat or a ship. So using what I know about those clue words and phrases, I predict that *buoy* is some kind of floating light that tells ships not to go there. Now I can go on and see if that prediction is accurate. So

I figured out the meaning of the word by myself by using clues and my experience to predict the meaning."

Scaffolded Assistance

Level 1: Extensive Teacher Help

Say something like:

"Now let's see if you can use context clues. I'll help you at first. Let's look at this sentence together [posts on chart paper]:

> The wind shook the poplar so hard that some of its leaves fell to the ground.

"Okay, *poplar* is a new word for us [circles it on the chart paper]. But let's see if we can use context to figure out its meaning. First we have to use words around the unknown word for clues. I'll read the sentence again. You listen for a clue toward the end of the sentence. Yes, *leaves* might be a clue [underlines it on the chart paper]. Let's think about what we already know about leaves. Where do we find leaves? Yes, we know from our own experience that leaves are found on trees. So, if a poplar's leaves were falling to the ground, can you predict what a poplar must be? See how you used your experience with the clue word *leaves* and predicted the meaning of the unknown word?"

Level 2: Less Teacher Help

Say something like:

"Let's listen to another sentence I made up, but this time I'm not going to provide as much help. The sentence is [posts the following]:

> The king laughed at the jokes and tricks performed by the jester.

"Look at the sentence again and tell me what word you don't know. Okay, if you don't know the word *jester*, we can use context clues to solve the problem. What do you do first? Yes, we look for clues. Is *king* a clue? Yes, and we know something about kings. And, yes, *jokes* is a clue, and *tricks* is a clue. So use your knowledge about kings, jokes, and tricks. What can you predict might be the meaning of *jester*? Yes, we might call them 'clowns.' As we listen to later sentences, we will check to see if 'clowns' makes sense."

Level 3: No Teacher Help

Once students appear to grasp the idea, read a sentence to them containing clues for an unknown word and ask students to tell you what it means and to describe for you how they figured it out.

Continued Application to Reading

The application in this example occurs when the group listens to the teacher read *Tornadoes* in preparation for contributing to a class manual on severe weather. As the four students listen, the teacher directs them to certain sentences and rereads them. For instance, she may direct them to the first page and the sentence containing the word *funnel* and have them tell her how they figured out the meaning of that word by using the clues "huge elephant's trunk" and "giant vacuum cleaner" to predict the meaning of *funnel*.

POST-LESSON CONSIDERATIONS

Post-Instruction Assessment

You will know students are ready to meet the standard for using context clues to determine word meaning if, after listening to you read the book *Tornadoes*, the students use the new words encountered in the text in their later class discussions about severe weather and if, in subsequent listening situations, the four students can state the meaning of the unknown words and describe how they used context clues to figure out the meaning of those words.

Links to Common Core Writing Standards

The second-grade Common Core standards include writing both narrative and informational text. In writing such text, students can be encouraged to include words that are likely to be new to their audience, but to also include around the new words some clues the audience can use to figure out the new word's meaning.

Example 15

Text Features
(CRAFT AND STRUCTURE—RI STANDARD 5)

BACKGROUND

Informational text makes use of a variety of text features, including tables of contents, glossaries, bold print, electronic menus, headings, and a variety of other features. Good readers use these features to locate needed information quickly.

> To teach text features, focus on two keys. First, students need to know that good readers do not always read informational text word-for-word, but instead use text features to find information without reading every word. Second, students need to know what specific fact or key bit of information they are looking for and read quickly (or skim the text) to find what they need.

The example provided here is based on the grade 2 Common Core standard *RI.2.5: Know and use various text feature (e.g., captions, bold print, subheadings, glossaries, indexes, electronic menus, icons) to locate key facts or information in a text efficiently.* The example assumes a hypothetical second-grade classroom.

> *Note for teachers of other grade levels:* For meeting this standard at other grade levels, adapt the following suggestions to your particular situation. For instance, when teaching to standard *RI.K.5: Identify the front cover, back cover, and title page of a book,* kindergarten teachers using a big book version of Maurice Sendak's *Where the Wild Things Are* (HarperCollins, 1963)

can explain those text features. Similarly, when teaching to standard *RI.3.5: Use text features and search tools (e.g., key words, sidebars, hyperlinks) to locate information relevant to a given topic efficiently*, third-grade teachers could use the Internet and an explanation similar to the one suggested here.

PRE-LESSON CONSIDERATIONS

Pre-Instruction Assessment

You will know students are not yet ready to meet this standard if, when locating facts in informational text, they read every word in the text and do not report using any kind of feature as a shortcut.

Large Conceptual Ideas You Can Reinforce during This Lesson

As you teach this lesson, look for opportunities to reinforce big understandings about reading such as:

- Informational text routinely includes features designed to help readers efficiently find specific kinds of information.
- It is not always necessary to read informational text word-for-word; in fact, the most efficient readers of informational text know what they are looking for before they start and use text features as shortcuts that eliminate the need to read everything.
- Informational text is important because answers to whatever questions we have can be found in informational text.

ORGANIZING FOR INSTRUCTION

Embedding Instruction in Reading for Purpose and Understanding

In this example, second-grade students have expressed concern about whales and the fact that they are endangered. Under the guidance of the teacher, they have initiated an Internet search for information that might help them understand the plight of whales and what could be done to save them from extinction. Because a few students have not met the standard for text features, the teacher decides to use the whale project as a vehicle for teaching them how to make efficient use of text features.

Ideas for Differentiating Instruction

One idea you could use if you were this teacher: Students not working with you on this standard choose a classroom center (some having computers, some having iPads, some having various kinds of informational text) and continue to search for information they could contribute to the class project on how to save the whales from extinction.

THE LESSON

Display, Post, or State the Objective

"By the end of this lesson, you will be able to find facts in informational text quickly by using text features such as headings and subheadings as clues and by reading just those sections of the text that are likely to provide the facts you are looking for."

Introducing the Lesson

Say something like:

> "Let's see if we can find out more about the plight of whales by looking at some Internet sites. But while we're doing that, I also want to teach you how to use clues in informational text to find out what we are looking for quickly and easily."

Stating the Secret to Doing It

Say something like:

> "There are two secrets to using text features to find factual information. First, you do not always have to read every single word in the text. In fact, really good readers often do not read every word in informational text. Second, you can use clues such as headings, subheadings, and picture captions to find what you are looking for more quickly."

Modeling the Thinking

Say something like:

"Let me show you how I use some of these shortcuts [finds a website (*www.animals.nationalgeographic.com*) and projects a text on the blue whale on her white board/smart board]. This website has text like most informational texts. But it also has some special stuff I can use as shortcuts to finding out what I want to know about whales. For instance, let's look at the first page. Without reading the text, I can find out how much whales eat just by looking at the caption. And over here on the side of the page we have a separate section called 'Fast Facts' which gives me all sorts of information I can find quickly. Captions like this one and side sections like this one are called 'text features,' and we can use them as shortcuts when we are looking for specific things in informational text."

Scaffolded Assistance

Level 1: Extensive Teacher Assistance

Say something like:

"Okay, let's see if we can use shortcuts like these to find out about whales being endangered. Let's look at this site [projects *www.npca. org* on the white board/smart board]. What do you see on this site that we could use as shortcuts in finding facts about whales? Let's look at the subheadings. Can we use them as shortcuts so that we don't have to read everything? We are interested in the fact that whales are endangered. Is there a subheading here that gives us a clue about where to look for information that might tell us more about whales being endangered? Yes, there's a heading labeled 'Threats.' Because we want to find out information about whales being endangered, we could skip some of the other text and go immediately to the subheading 'Threats' and see if that gives us more information that we don't yet have."

Level 2: Less Teacher Help

Say something like:

> "Okay, now let's look at another site and see if we can use features such
> as headings, subheadings, and captions to find information about
> whales being endangered [searches the website *www.livescience.*
> *com* for information on whales and projects a section on the Orca
> whale on her white board/smart board]. There are lots of headings
> we can use here. We're looking for information about whales being
> endangered. So let's look down through the headings shown here.
> Is there a heading you could go to quickly to find information on
> whales being endangered? We see a heading on 'what they eat,' a
> heading for 'where they live,' and a heading for 'odd facts.' But is
> there a heading for 'endangered' or for anything that might tell us
> about whales being endangered? No. So, how have the headings
> helped us? Yes, we have found out that this site may not give us what
> we need about whales being endangered so we have saved time—we
> don't have to read the whole text."

Level 3: No Teacher Help

The teacher projects another site [*www.animal.discovery.com*] on the
smart board. She directs students to examine the text to see if there
is information they can use about whales being endangered, and she
reminds them to use the headings and other features to make it easier to
locate the information they want.

Continued Application to Reading

The teacher will continue to remind students to use text features such as
captions and headings to help them find needed information quickly in
informational text about whales, as well as when they read other informational text on other topics.

POST-LESSON CONSIDERATIONS

Post-Instruction Assessment

You will know students are ready to meet the standard for using text features if, when reading informational text, you observe them using headings, bold print, captions, and other features to find the information they need quickly and efficiently.

Links to Common Core Writing Standards

The Common Core writing standards for the second grade list the following standard: *W.2.2: Write informative/explanatory texts in which they introduce a topic, use facts and definitions to develop points, and provide a concluding statement or section.* When writing such texts, students should be encouraged to insert features into their writing of informational text that they have used in reading, such as headings, subheadings, and other features that would help their readers as they search for particular kinds of information.

Example 16

Text Structure

(CRAFT AND STRUCTURE—RI STANDARD 5)

BACKGROUND

Well-written informational text has an internal structure that aids the reader in comprehending the text. Some of those aids are fairly obvious text features such as headings, captions, and bold print (see Example 15). Other text structures are less obvious and represent the way the information is organized. For instance, information can be presented as a chronology, as a comparison, as a cause–effect, or as a problem/solution. When readers are sensitive to how a particular piece of informational text is structured, they can comprehend it more efficiently.

> To teach text structure, first establish that authors organize the information in ways that will most directly and clearly convey their meaning. Then students must be made aware of what structure to look for and use their predicting–monitoring–repredicting skills with that structure in mind.

The example provided here is based on the Common Core standard *RI.4.5: Describe the overall structure (e.g., chronology, comparison, cause/effect, problem/solution) of events, ideas, concepts or information in a text or part of a text.* It assumes a hypothetical fourth-grade classroom where the teacher is teaching students to recognize comparison text structures.

Note to teachers of other grade levels: The following suggestions can be adapted when teaching other kinds of text structure or when teaching text structure at other grade levels. For instance, seventh-grade social studies teachers using the textbook *The Pacific Northwest: Past, Present and Future* (Directed Media, 1993) would use the same basic explanation to help students distinguish among and use text structures when teaching standard *RI.7.5: Analyze the structure an author uses to organize a text, including how the major sections contribute to the whole and to the development of the ideas.*

PRE-LESSON CONSIDERATIONS

Pre-Instruction Assessment

You will know students are not ready to meet the standard for text structure if, when presented with a text having an obvious structure, they are unable to name the structure and predict how the information will be presented.

Large Conceptual Ideas You Can Reinforce during This Lesson

As you teach this lesson, look for opportunities to reinforce big understandings about reading such as the following:

- The best writers structure what they write in ways that most clearly convey the information, and the best readers use what they know about how writers structure text to more easily locate the information they need.
- Good readers use text structure to quickly locate information, and they often do so without reading every word in the text.
- Being a good comprehender means anticipating in advance things like text structure so that information can be located quickly and easily.
- Various subject matter tends to employ certain kinds of text structure (e.g., social studies tends to use chronology when the topic is history; science tends to use problem/solution for experiments).

ORGANIZING FOR INSTRUCTION

Embedding Instruction in Reading for Purpose and Understanding

This example is set in a fourth-grade classroom where students are pursuing a science unit on weather, with their ultimate goal being to use what they learn to predict the weather for a week. In the course of the study, students raise questions about climate change. In preparing to answer those questions, the teacher decides to have some students pursue their questions about climate change in peer groups using classroom computers and iPads while she meets with a small group that has not met the standard for text structure.

Ideas for Differentiating Instruction

One idea you could use if you were this teacher: At the beginning of the project on climate change, the teacher led the students in the K-W-L technique in which they generated statements about what they already know about climate change and what they want to learn; students not working with you on this standard work in peer groups; each group of students selects a question to answer from the list of K-W-L questions posed earlier and uses classroom computers and iPads to gather information to answer those questions.

THE LESSON

Display, Post, or State the Objective

"By the end of this lesson, you will be able to describe one way in which informational text can be structured, and you will be able to use that knowledge to find the information you need."

Introducing the Lesson

Say something like:

"You have raised some questions about climate change because you may be thinking that climate and weather are almost the same. Actually, they are quite different. We're going to read some informational text from the Internet to determine how they are different, but I also want to show you how you can use text structures to help you find out what you want to know."

Stating the Secret to Doing It

Say something like:

> "To use informational text well, we should be looking to see if it is structured in a way to help you. If you know how a text is structured, you can more easily find the information you want."

Modeling the Thinking

Say something like:

> "Let me show you how I do it, using this first piece of informational text I found on the Internet [projects on her white board/smart board a text on 'climate concepts' from *www.epa.gov*]. When I look at this text, I first keep in mind what I'm looking for. I want to find out how 'climate' and 'weather' are different. Then I look at the text to see if it has a structure that will help me find the answer. When I look at this text, I see a heading for 'weather versus climate' so I expect that this text will be structured as a comparison. As I start to read, I am predicting I will find 'weather' and 'climate' compared. I begin reading, and that is what I find. It says that weather happens over hours or days but that climate happens over years."

Scaffolded Assistance

Level 1: Extensive Teacher Help

Say something like:

> "Now let's look at another piece of Internet text, but now I want you to help me as we try to find out more information about the difference between 'weather' and 'climate' [projects on her white board/ smart board a link from *kidsnewsroom.org*]. What do you see when you look at this text? Is it structured in a way that will help us find what we're looking for? Yes, the title is 'Climate and Weather,' so this text is probably set up as a comparison. So it is structured to

help me answer my question. We can predict that we'll find what we need here, and so we begin looking for a comparison. Do you find one? Yes, this site says, like the last one, that weather is for hours or days and that climate goes over many years. But it also gives us other information. It distinguishes, for instance, weather from climate by describing climate as what it is usually like where you live (i.e., it's a mild climate, or it's a snowy climate)."

Level 2: Less Teacher Help

Say something like:

"Now let's try one with you doing more of the work [projects on her white board/smart board a site from *tiki.oneworld.net*]. This piece of text looks a little different from the others. But can you examine it and see if it has a structure that will help you? Yes, it starts right out with the questions 'What is climate? What is weather?' So what can you do as a reader? What do you expect to find? Yes, you expect to find a comparison. So you make the prediction that you will find a comparison of 'weather' and 'climate.' Do you find that? Yes, so the structure of the text helped you more easily find the information you needed."

Level 3: No Teacher Help

The teacher projects a different site [another one from *www.epa.gov*] on her smart board. She has the students examine the structure, determine if it is a comparison, and describe how they would engage with the text if it is structured as a comparison.

Continued Application to Reading

As students continue to pursue the weather unit, as well as other units in both science and social studies, they will encounter text structured as comparison but will also encounter texts structured in other ways. As these text structures are recognized, the teacher continues to develop an understanding of how knowledge of text structure helps us comprehend text more efficiently.

POST-LESSON CONSIDERATIONS

Post-Instruction Assessment

You will know students are ready to meet the standard for text structure if, when encountering informational text, they recognize the way the text is structured and can describe how the text structure helps them find the information they need.

Links to Common Core Writing Standards

The Common Core's fourth-grade writing standards include *W.4.2: Write informative/explanatory texts to examine a topic and convey ideas and information clearly.* Students are aided in achieving this writing standard if what they learned about text structures in reading is incorporated into their writing, so that what they write is structured in a way that most clearly communicates the desired information.

Example 17

Analyzing Positions and Views
(CRAFT AND STRUCTURE—RI STANDARD 6)

BACKGROUND

This example is representative of the Common Core's standard requiring students to distinguish between different sources of information. In the early grades, the focus is on distinguishing between information provided by authors and illustrators; in later grades, the focus is on distinguishing between information from contrasting points of view.

> To teach this standard, the usual comprehension strategies of predicting, monitoring, and repredicting are employed to identify various positions and views. Additionally, however, students must then compare the positions and identify similarities and differences.

The example provided here is based on Common Core standard *RI.5.6: Analyze multiple accounts of the same event or topic, noting important similarities and differences in the point of view they represent.* A hypothetical fifth-grade situation is used to illustrate how to teach to this standard.

> *Note for teachers of other grade levels:* For meeting this standard at other grade levels, adapt the following suggestions to your particular situation. For instance, a kindergarten teacher could use a less complex text such as Robert McCloskey's *Make Way for Ducklings* (Viking Press, 1941) and explain in similar ways when teaching to *RI.K.6: Name the author and illustrator of a text and define the role of each in presenting the ideas or information in a text.*

PRE-LESSON CONSIDERATIONS

Pre-Instruction Assessment

You will know students are not ready to meet the standard for analyzing positions and views if, when discussing informational text representing two or more perspectives on a particular event, you observe that students are unable to answer questions about how the two positions are similar or different.

Large Conceptual Ideas You Can Reinforce during This Lesson

As you teach this lesson, look for opportunities to reinforce large understandings about reading such as the following:

- Readers actively construct meaning—it does not happen without effort.
- The predicting–monitoring–repredicting cycle is not a matter of guessing wildly—it is a matter of constructing thoughtful hypotheses based on the cues provided in the text.
- All comprehension requires inferring what the author may have meant and then confirming or rejecting that inference as more information becomes available.
- Different writers will write differently about the same subject because each one is operating from a different set of background experiences, which causes them to have a different point of view.
- It is important to consider the author's credentials and goals when analyzing positions and views.
- Being able to analyze positions and views is very important in the Information Age where different perspectives and points of view are a daily event.

ORGANIZING FOR INSTRUCTION

Embedding Instruction in Reading for Purpose and Understanding

This example is set in fifth grade and assumes students are studying the settling of the western part of the United States in social studies class. They have become particularly interested in the conflict between pioneer settlers and Native Americans and have initiated a project in which the goal is to understand the positions of both groups. As a part of this project, they have read both the description of Custer's Last Stand in their social studies book and newspaper accounts from that time. The majority of the class is going to read Paul Goble's *Red Hawk's Account of Custer's Last Stand* (University of Nebraska Press, 1992) independently, while the teacher uses the same text with a small group of students who have not met the standard for analyzing positions and views.

Ideas for Differentiating Instruction

One idea you could use if you were this teacher: Students not working with you on this standard will read *Red Hawk's Account of Custer's Last Stand* independently, using a graphic organizer prepared by the teacher to guide them in analyzing the differences in the positions taken by Red Hawk and those taken by the newspapers reporting on the battle.

THE LESSON

Post, Display, or State the Objective

"By the end of this lesson, you will be able to identify the point of view of the newspaper reports of Custer's Last Stand and how it is similar or different from the point of view presented in *Red Hawk's Account of Custer's Last Stand*."

Introducing the Lesson

Say something like:

"We have been studying the points of view of both the pioneers who settled the American West and the Native Americans who came in conflict with the settlers. Part of that conflict is reflected in battles such as Custer's Last Stand. Yesterday, we read about that event in our social studies book, and then we read some of the original newspaper reports of that battle. Today, we're going to read a Native American's report of the same battle. As part of our project to understand the positions of the settlers and the Native Americans, we will compare the two accounts of the battle to see how their points of view differ."

Stating the Secret to Doing It

Say something like:

> "To do this, you must first use your predicting–monitoring–repredicting skills to determine what Red Hawk's view is. Then you must set Red Hawk's view side by side with what we learned yesterday from the newspaper reports, looking first for what is similar in what they say in both accounts and then for what is different in what they say from one account to the other."

Modeling the Thinking

Say something like:

> "Let me show you how to do this using the first part of Red Hawk's account. As I begin reading, I make a prediction about what I'm going to find out. I say to myself, 'I know Red Hawk is a Native American, so I think I'm going to find out that they were looking for a battle with Custer.' As I read along, I find out that that is not the case. The Indians were gathered in a village at the Little Big Horn for other reasons. I say to myself, 'Was this the same as what was reported in the newspaper or different?' To help me compare these two views, I'm going to write two columns on a piece of paper and put Red Hawk's view in one column and what the newspapers said about Custer's view in the other column. Now I can look at them side by side. When I do that, I can see that the newspaper reports say the Indians were looking for a fight but that Red Hawk says they were not. When I do this comparison, I can see that their points of view were different. By identifying the two views and comparing one with the other, I can decide whether their views were the same or different."

Scaffolded Assistance

Level 1: Extensive Teacher Help

Say something like:

> "All right, let's try one together. This time we won't actually write down what we find in columns on a piece of paper—we'll just set

them side by side in our minds. Let's read to see what Red Hawk is saying about the battle. What are you finding out? Yes, Red Hawk says that the Indians attacked and that many of the soldiers ran away. So let's set this side by side with what the newspapers say happened. Yes, the newspapers say all the soldiers stood fast and made a last stand. Are these two views the same or different? By setting them side by side in our minds, we can determine whether they both had the same point of view or different points of view."

Level 2: Less Teacher Help

Say something like:

"On page 5 of Red Hawk's account, there is a quote from Sitting Bull that says, 'I tell no lies about dead men. Those men who came with Long Hair were as good men as ever fought.' What is he saying about Custer's soldiers? Yes, he's saying that they were brave and that he admired them. Now let's look at what the newspapers said about the Indians. Were the newspapers positive or negative about the Indians. Yes, what they said sounds negative. So let's set these two views side by side in our minds. Do they both view their enemies the same way?"

Level 3: No Teacher Help

As students progress through the remaining sections of Red Hawk's account, remind them to use their predicting–monitoring–repredicting cycle to determine his perspective and to then look for similarities and differences in how other accounts of Custer's Last Stand were the same and different.

Continued Application to Reading

As students continue to pursue their project of understanding the positions of the settlers and of the Native Americans, they will be reading other informational text. In those situations, continue to remind students to use what they have learned about analyzing positions and views.

POST-LESSON CONSIDERATIONS

Post-Instruction Assessment

You will know students are ready to meet the standard for analyzing positions and views if students can answer questions requiring them to identify different positions or views and can state whether they are similar or different and what makes them so.

Links to Common Core Writing Standards

The Common Core specifies standard W.5.1a as follows: *Introduce a topic or text clearly, state an opinion and create an organizational structure in which ideas are logically grouped to support the writer's purpose.* This is a "point of view" task and in that way is similar to the above reading standard. Students will be aided in "logically grouping" their ideas in support of an opinion if they can draw on experiences in reading in which positions and views were logically grouped and easy to compare with other positions.

Example 18

Using Graphic Information

(INTEGRATION OF KNOWLEDGE AND IDEAS— RI STANDARD 7)

BACKGROUND

Informational text often conveys meaning through illustrations, diagrams, maps, photographs, graphs, time lines, and other forms of graphic information. To be able to comprehend informational text well, readers must be able to use graphic information to understand and clarify text meaning.

> To teach graphic meaning, start by explaining the purpose of the particular graphic, much as you teach the meaning of content words (see Example 13). Once students understand what the particular graphic is, you must show them how to combine the graphic with the information in the text to gain a fuller understanding of what is being conveyed.

The teaching example provided here is based on the third-grade standard: *RI.3.7: Use information gained from illustrations (e.g., maps, photographs) and the words in the text to demonstrate understanding of the text (e.g., where, when, why, and how key events occur).* It assumes a hypothetical third-grade classroom.

> *Note for teachers of other grade levels:* The suggestions provided for this standard can be applied at other grade levels. For instance, a kindergarten teacher reading Ezra Jack Keats's *The Snowy Day* (Viking Juvenile, 1962) to the class would use basically the same explanation when teaching *RI.K.7:*

With prompting and support, describe the relationship between illustrations and the text in which they appear (e.g., what person, place, thing, or idea in the text an illustration depicts.

PRE-LESSON CONSIDERATIONS

Pre-Instruction Assessment

You will know students are not ready to meet the standard for using graphic information if, during discussion of a text, they cannot provide an explanation of how the graphic clarifies the text meaning.

Large Conceptual Ideas You Can Reinforce during This Lesson

As you teach this lesson, look for opportunities to reinforce big understandings about reading such as the following:

- Meaning can be communicated by illustrations and other kinds of graphic information as well as by words.
- Informational text often uses graphic information because the content is often more complex and harder to understand with just words alone.
- Good comprehenders use all available clues when reading.

ORGANIZING FOR INSTRUCTION

Embedding Instruction in Reading for Purpose and Understanding

This third-grade classroom is engaged in a science unit on sound. They are using what they are learning to make their own musical instruments so they can provide a concert for the kindergarten class. They have been using various textual sources, including the Internet, to gain information about how sound works. Now they are ready to read about how musical instruments produce sound. The electronic text has many illustrations, which most of the class can use effectively. However, some students cannot yet meet the standard for using graphic information, so the teacher takes this opportunity to form a temporary group of those students and to teach them how to use accompanying graphic information as they read Internet information about musical instruments.

Ideas for Differentiating Instruction

One idea you could use if you were this teacher: Students not working with you on this standard will work in groups—one for stringed instruments, one for woodwinds, one for percussion, and one for brass instruments—and use Internet sources to investigate how these various instruments produce music.

THE LESSON

Display, Post, or State the Objective

"By the end of this lesson, you will be able to tell how illustrations combined with the words in the text contribute to your understanding about sound and musical instruments."

Introducing the Lesson

Say something like:

> "Now that we've learned some of the basics about how sound works, we are ready to begin reading to find out how musical instruments produce sound. We will use this information when we make our own instruments for the concert we're going to perform for the kindergartners. While we want to find out information about musical instruments, we are also going to use illustrations in books and from the Internet to help us understand what the words in the text are saying."

Stating the Secret to Doing It

Say something like:

> "In order to use illustrations to help us understand text, we need first to know the purpose of the illustration and how it is designed to help us. Then we need to read the text and examine the illustration, combine them, and explain what the text and the illustration together are telling us."

Modeling the Thinking

Say something like:

> "Let me show you how to combine illustrations and the words in the text. I'll show you first and then we'll look at some information from

the Internet and you can help me. Let's start with this book [holds up the *How Things Work* Encyclopedia; DK Publishing, 2010]. On page 88 of this book, there is text on making sound with a drum. When I read the text, I only find that it says, 'Any object that vibrates can make a sound' and 'Sound is made up of waves of vibrations moving through the air.' But that doesn't tell me anything about how the drum makes sound. To find out how the drum makes sound, I have to look at the illustration. The illustration shows someone tapping on a drum. And there is a little note on the drum that says, 'Hitting with a drum stick makes the drum vibrate which makes the air vibrate.' When I put what the text says together with what I learned from the illustration, I now know how the drum produces sound."

Scaffolded Assistance

Level 1: Extensive Teacher Help

Say something like:

"Let's start with this Internet site [projects *scienceforkidsblog* on her white board/smart board]. This site is telling how sound is made by vibrations and that kids can make their own kazoo and have a kazoo orchestra. What do the words in the text say about how to do it? Yes, it says that if you blow through the straw there will be no vibration but that there will be vibrations if you 'cut the straw into straw horns.' I'm not sure what that means. So now look at the illustration. What do you see there? Yes, the illustration makes it clear that to make a kazoo you have to pinch the end of the straw before you blow through it in order to get a vibration. This is a good illustration of how meaning is clarified by using the illustrations."

Level 2: Less Teacher Help

Say something like:

"Okay, let's look at this website [projects *pbskids.org* on her white board/smart board]. This is explaining how string instruments work and is a good example of how illustrations help us make sense out of text. Let's read what the text says. Yes, it's saying that the amount of tension you put on a string determines the vibration and sound. But now look at the illustration. What does it show? Yes, there are two strings moving back and forth, one slowly and one quickly. What do we learn from looking at the illustration? Yes, we can see from the illustration that the slowly vibrating string is making a lower note and the faster vibrating string is making a higher note. Can you see how looking at the illustration clarified our understanding of how stringed instruments work?"

Level 3: No Teacher Help

At this point, the teacher puts up more websites and has students work together in pairs. Each group reads the text, looks at the illustration, and explains how the illustration clarified what the words were saying.

Continued Application to Reading

Following this lesson, students will continue to read informational text on sound, on how musical instruments make sound, and on how to make their own instruments. The teacher will remind them to use what they know about using illustrations to help them understand what the text is saying.

POST-LESSON CONSIDERATIONS

Post-Instruction Assessment

You will know students are ready to meet the Common Core standard for using graphic information if, during subsequent discussions of informational text, students can explain how they used the illustrations to clarify the meaning of the text.

Links to Common Core Writing Standards

The Common Core specifies that students should be writing informational and explanatory text. Once they have learned to use graphic information when reading, they should be encouraged to insert graphic information into the informational/explanatory texts they are composing. Given the unit on sound in this example, for instance, students could write such text on how their respective musical instruments make sound and provide an accompanying graphic to illustrate it more clearly.

Example 19

Evaluating Supportive Evidence
(INTEGRATION OF KNOWLEDGE AND IDEAS— RI STANDARD 8)

BACKGROUND

Ensuring that students do "close reading" is a consistent concern of the Common Core. "Close reading" means reading and interpreting text meaning in thorough and analytical ways, as opposed to making superficial or casual "guesses" about text meaning.

A particularly important type of "close reading" is the ability to evaluate positions taken by authors. It requires careful analysis of the reasons and evidence provided to support an argument, and requires readers to make a judgment about the relative validity of an author's position.

Being able to evaluate an author's position is particularly important in today's Information Age. We are constantly being bombarded in listening, viewing, and reading situations with information designed to influence us in one way or another. Consequently, evaluating text is a crucial comprehension strategy.

To teach evaluating, focus students first on using their predicting–monitoring–repredicting skills to determine the position the author is taking. Then readers must locate the evidence the author offers in support of the position and, using one's own logic and background knowledge, make a judgment about whether the points the author makes are supported by the evidence offered.

The example provided here is based on the Common Core standard for sixth grade: *RI.6.8: Trace and evaluate the argument and specific claims in a text, distinguishing claims that are supported by reasons and evidence from claims that are not.* It assumes a hypothetical sixth-grade classroom.

Note to teachers of other grade levels: The suggestions provided here for a sixth-grade class can be adapted and applied in much the same form in other grades. For instance, a second-grade teacher using the big book *The Wheels on the Bus,* by Maryann Kovalski (Trumpet Club, 1987), would similarly have students focus on the author's statements and have them use their experience to make a judgment when teaching to standard *RI.2.8: Describe how reasons support specific points the author makes in a text.*

PRE-LESSON CONSIDERATIONS

Pre-Instruction Assessment

You will know students are not ready to meet the Common Core standard for evaluating supportive evidence if students passively accept what they read in books or if they are unable to make reference to evidence when stating whether they agree or disagree with an author's argument.

Large Conceptual Ideas You Can Reinforce during This Lesson

As you teach this lesson, look for opportunities to reinforce big understandings about reading such as the following:

- Informational text is not necessarily factual or true and must be evaluated.
- It is acceptable to disagree with an author's opinions.
- Making judgments about the validity of text is an important part of being a good reader.
- Analyzing text requires proactive, assertive thinking.
- Evaluating text is particularly important in the age of the Internet, blogs, twitters, and multiple other sources that all want to convince you that their positions are the right ones.

ORGANIZING FOR INSTRUCTION

Embedding Instruction in Reading for Purpose and Understanding

This example is set in a sixth-grade classroom. The school is located in a city that is debating a referendum to fluorinate the municipal water supply. The debate has been vigorous among the city's citizenry, and, consequently, the students have been talking about it. The teacher decides that, given the pro- and con- arguments flying back and forth in the newspaper, this is an opportunity to teach students how to evaluate the validity of arguments and the use of supportive evidence. She initiates a project that involves reading and evaluating the various arguments for and against fluorination that will culminate in a classroom debate in which students compose their own arguments, supported by evidence and reasons. Students who have met this standard work in small groups to analyze various newspaper articles for and against fluoridation. Those students who have not yet met the standard for evaluation work with the teacher in a temporary group.

Ideas for Differentiating Instruction

One idea you could use if you were this teacher: Students not working with you on this standard work in small groups and analyze news articles on fluoridation, using as a guide a list of typical propaganda characteristics. The task is to identify if and when propaganda techniques have been used in the news articles.

THE LESSON

Display, Post, or State the Objective

"By the end of this lesson, you will be able to read a newspaper article or letter to the editor that takes a position on the fluorination debate, and identify for each article or letter whether the reasons and evidence provided support the point being made."

Introducing the Lesson

Say something like:

> "In order for us to intelligently debate the fluorination issue, we need to be able to read what people are saying, both for and against, and be able to evaluate whether the reasons they give for their position supports the point being made. Because the fluorination issue is so current right now, I will show you how to evaluate supportive evidence using some *USA Today* editorials on other topics that are not so close to home. Then you will begin reading what is being written in the newspaper about fluorination and make judgments about the arguments being made."

Stating the Secret to Doing It

Say something like:

> "The secret to making judgments about an argument's supportive evidence is to look first at the position being taken (Is it pro? Is it con?), then look at the reasons the person gives to support his position, and then use your own background knowledge to make a judgment about whether the evidence presented supports the argument."

Modeling the Thinking

Say something like:

> "Let me show you how I do it. Let's look first at this set of two editorials in *USA Today* on a debate over a new law requiring voter registration [uses a document camera to display the two editorials]. The first thing I do is read each article to determine what the author's position is. The first article is arguing against requiring potential voters to register in advance of elections [underlines the point in the article]. The other is arguing for requiring potential voters to register in advance [underlines that point]. So now I have to look at the evidence being presented on each side. I look to see if the first presents any evidence. I find that the author reports a research study

showing that requiring early registration suppresses voter turnout [underlines the point]. Now I look at the other article. I see that the author is the person who wrote the law and that he says objections to the law are untrue. But he offers no study or evidence to support that claim. So now I look at the two arguments. One offers the results of a research study to support his argument; the other says his position is correct but offers no evidence. In my experience, the results of a study are more reliable than an opinion unsupported by evidence. The first author uses evidence to support his position, but the second one uses only his personal opinion."

Scaffolded Assistance

Level 1: Extensive Teacher Help

Say something like:

"Okay, let's look at another set of editorials on another issue. These two articles are debating whether the U.S. should vote in one way or another in an upcoming session of the United Nations. So let's look at these articles together [displays them as before]. What is the first article arguing for? Yes, this article wants the U.S. to vote for the resolution. How about the second article? Yes, it wants the U.S. to vote against the resolution. So now we have to look at the evidence offered by the two sides. Let's look at the first article. What do we find there to support the argument to vote for the resolution? The author points out that there are disadvantages to voting for the resolution but in the ending paragraph says it should be done. Is there any reasons why this would be the right thing to do? No, I don't see any. Now let's look at the other article. Are there reasons given for not voting for the resolutions? Yes, the article quotes two important political leaders and one general, all of whom say the resolution will not solve the problem. So if we set the two articles side by side, what does our experience tell us about the strength of the two arguments. Yes, we see that one offers no reasons while the other offers the opinions of people perceived to be experts. The second argument is better supported."

Level 2: Less Teacher Help

Say something like:

> "Okay, now let's look at another set of editorials, but this time you must do more of the work. What do we do first? Yes, we have to read to see what each article is saying. So what do you find? Yes, one article is arguing for the death penalty for all murder cases, and the other is arguing for doing away with the death penalty in all cases. So now look at the reasons and evidence that each offers to support the argument. What does the first article offer as support? What does the second offer as support? Yes, the first says all murderers are bad, all deserve to die, and we cannot afford to be soft on murderers. The second points to several cases in which persons accused of murder have later been found to be innocent, and the death penalty should not be used. So now we have to decide whose argument is the strongest. Which one offered evidence? Is saying all murderers are bad evidence or opinion? Is saying that in some cases the wrong person is sentenced to death evidence or opinion? In this case, it doesn't seem that either side is offering much evidence. But do you think the second one is the stronger argument because at least it points to some cases that support not using the death penalty? So even though both arguments offer few reasons, the second one may be stronger simply because it does offer at least a little evidence."

Level 3: No Teacher Help

The teacher presents another two articles arguing for who is responsible for acid rain and what should be done about it. Students are given the two articles, and, working in pairs, they identify the arguments, assess the evidence offered in support, and make a judgment about which supportive evidence is most compelling.

Continued Application to Reading

Once students have demonstrated an understanding of how to evaluate supporting evidence, the teacher has them read the arguments appearing in the local newspaper and in letters to the editor regarding the debate on fluorination of the city's water supply. They analyze each one and report on how the author uses (or fails to use) reasons and evidence in supporting the points being made.

POST-LESSON CONSIDERATIONS

Post-Instruction Assessment

You will know students are ready to meet the Common Core standard for evaluating supporting evidence if, in reading text about this fluorination project and in reading texts in the future, they make statements about the degree to which authors support their arguments with reasons and evidence.

Links to Common Core Writing Standards

The Common Core sixth-grade standards for writing specify writing argumentative text (e.g., *W.6.1: write arguments to support claims with clear reasons and relevant evidence*). Students tend to get better at both evaluating supportive evidence in text they read and in writing text with supportive evidence if the two standards are integrated together. In the above example, for instance, students learn to evaluate evidence regarding the fluorination debate and then for their own classroom debate they write their own position statements supported by evidence.

Example 20

Synthesizing

(INTEGRATION OF KNOWLEDGE AND IDEAS—
RI STANDARD 9)

BACKGROUND

To *synthesize* means to combine or integrate several ideas into a single idea. In the Information Age, we are constantly faced with multiple sources of information. Being literate in the 21st century means being able to combine multiple sources of information. That is, to speak or write knowledgeably about a topic or issue, readers must be able to integrate several ideas into a single understanding.

The Common Core emphasizes synthesizing of ideas and text across all grade levels. First graders are expected to . . . *identify basic similarities in and differences between two texts on the same topic . . . (RI.K.9)*, while seventh graders are expected to . . . *analyze how two or more authors writing about the same topic shape their presentations of key information by emphasizing different evidence or advancing different interpretations of facts . . . (RI.7.9)*. At all levels, synthesizing requires readers to determine similarities and differences in text messages and to then combine the two messages together into a single message.

To teach synthesizing, first remind students to use their predicting–monitoring–repredicting skills to determine the content of information sources and then show them how to combine the information to create a message that includes all sources.

Synthesizing is difficult to teach because it requires readers to employ several prerequisites. In addition to the fundamental comprehension strategy of predicting–monitoring–repredicting, readers must identify key details (see Example 1), compare and contrast (see Example 10), and do careful analysis (see Example 17).

The teaching example provided here is based on the fourth-grade standard (*RI.4.9: Integrate information from two texts on the same topic in order to write or speak about the subject knowledgeably*). It assumes a hypothetical fourth-grade classroom.

Note to teachers of other grade levels: The suggestions described here for teaching synthesizing to fourth graders is basically the same as one would use to explain synthesizing at any grade level. For instance, first graders working on *RI.1.9*, which focuses on identifying basic similarities and differences between two texts on the same topic, could use the big book *Humphrey the Wrong Way Whale* (by Gare Thompson; Scholastic, 1989) and an Internet description of whales in water parks from Wikipedia and engage in the same process of using predicting to locate details in the two texts and then setting the texts side by side so the ideas from both can be combined.

PRE-LESSON CONSIDERATIONS

Pre-Instruction Assessment

You will know students are not ready to meet the Common Core standard for synthesizing if you observe that students cannot compose a statement in which information from two different texts is combined into a single message.

Large Conceptual Ideas You Can Reinforce during This Lesson

As you teach this lesson, look for opportunities to reinforce big understandings about reading such as the following:

- Information about a common topic can come from a variety of sources.
- In an age where we are assaulted with tons of information, it is important to be able to combine ideas from many sources.
- Reading is a construction process in which meaning is created, especially when we are combining ideas from multiple sources.

ORGANIZING FOR INSTRUCTION

Embedding Instruction in Reading for Purpose and Understanding

In this fourth-grade classroom, students are engaged in a long-term project on famous women in American history. Consequently, the class is reading biographies of famous women, with the long-term goal being the presentation of a program at a school assembly on the character traits that distinguish famous American women. Working in small groups, the students have each selected a woman they want to study, with each group responsible for reporting to the class on what they found out about their particular woman's character traits. Since each group must read at least two biographies of the woman of their choice, the teacher plans a whole-group lesson on how to synthesize information from two texts. She has chosen to use two biographies about Helen Keller for her lesson: Laurie Lawlor's *Helen Keller: Rebellious Spirit*, Holiday House, 2001; and Leslie Garrett's *Helen Keller,®* DK Publishing, 2004.

Ideas for Differentiating Instruction

One idea you could use if you were this teacher: This example assumes a whole-class lesson on synthesizing. But at the end of that whole-class lesson, when the teacher does the post-instruction assessment, she will find that some students still need help in meeting the standard. At that point, she would group those students and provide an additional lesson on synthesizing, while the rest of the class would work in their groups to continue writing the biographies of the woman they have chosen.

THE LESSON

Display, Post, or State the Objective

"By the end of this lesson, you will be able to combine ideas from two biographies into a single message you can use when you report to the class about the character traits that distinguish your woman."

Introducing the Lesson

Say something like:

> "Your groups are responsible for reporting back to the class about the character traits you think distinguishes your woman. But you each must read two biographies about your woman, and any two biographies typically have different things to say. So today we'll learn to combine the ideas from two biographies into a single message we can then use in our report to the class. We call this combining 'synthesizing.'"

The Secret to Doing It

Say something like:

> "Synthesizing is difficult because we have to use strategies we learned earlier as well as a new strategy. First, we have to use what we've learned about predicting–monitoring–repredicting to find out what the messages are in each of the two biographies. Then we have to compare and contrast the ideas from the two biographies. Finally, we have to combine the different ideas from the two biographies into a single message we can use when we report back to the class."

Modeling the Thinking

Say something like:

> "Since none of you chose to do a biography on Helen Keller, I'll use her as my biography. Let me show you how to do it using these two biographies of her [holds up Laurie Lawlor's *Helen Keller: Rebellious Spirit* and *Leslie Garrett's Helen Keller*]. Let's look first at this biography [uses a document camera to show the pages of Lawlor's book to the whole class]. As we read the first three pages, we find out that Helen Keller wanted very much to be accepted like everyone else, but we also find out some things about how difficult it was for her and that she developed a 'quiet, stubborn persistence' in order to deal with the difficulty. Now let's look at this biography [projects the

Garrett book for the class to see]. This book also says on the first few pages that Helen Keller wanted to be treated like everyone else. But it says nothing about her being stubborn or persistent. So if we set these two sections side by side, we can see that there are similarities but there is also a difference. So now we have to combine the two statements. I take the part both books agree on (that she wanted to be like everyone else) and then add in the different idea from Lawlor's book. When I combine the two, I have a statement that looks like this [writes on the board 'Helen Keller wanted to be treated like everyone else but it was hard and it was a struggle for her. In order to be who she wanted to be, she had to develop a stubborn attitude that allowed her to persist despite the difficulty']. So by combining the information from both biographies, I have a single message that captures the meaning from both."

Scaffolded Assistance

Level 1: Extensive Teacher Help

Say something like:

"Okay, let's read on in these two Helen Keller biographies but now you must help me and do some of the work. As we read further in the Lawlor biography, what do we find as we get to pages 8 and 9? Yes, we find information about Helen when she was older, and on pages 10 and 11 we find out about her home and her family. Now let's look at the Garrett biography. When we get to pages 14 and 15, what do we find out? Yes, this is all about Helen when she was very young, and we learn that she was mischievous. So when we set the two books side by side and compare the messages in both, we see that they are similar in many ways but different in other ways. What is similar in these two sections? And what is different? Yes, the Garrett biography provides a lot more information about Helen as a very young child, but the Lawlor book does not. So can we make a statement that combines both? Yes, saying 'Helen lived in a small town in Alabama with her family, but she was very mischievous as a young child.' So we have synthesized the information from both biographies."

Level 2: Less Teacher Help

Say something like:

> "Okay, let's continue reading the two biographies, but now you must do most of the work. In the Garrett biography, what is the message we find on pages 16 and 17? Yes, we very quickly find out about Helen going to see Alexander Graham Bell for help and how he helped find a teacher for Helen. Now let's look at the description of the same incident in the Lawlor biography. Does it tell basically the same story? Yes, but the Lawlor one is quite different. How is it different? Set them side by side in your mind. What can you say that would synthesize the two descriptions of the meeting with Dr. Bell? Yes, there's a lot more detail in the Lawlor biography. So we could combine the two by saying that Helen went to Dr. Bell for help (which is true for both biographies) but then we can add detail from the Lawlor book about how difficult it was."

Level 3: No Teacher Help

The teacher could direct students to the two descriptions of Annie Sullivan (pages 18 and 19 in the Garrett biography and pages 30 and 31 in the Lawlor biography). There are similarities and differences in the descriptions of Annie, so students could set the two descriptions side by side, compare and contrast what is said, and come up with a statement that combines the two into a single message.

Continued Application to Reading

The immediate application of this lesson will occur as the students return to their groups, read the biographies of the women they have chosen, and compose statements that combine information from both for later use when reporting to the class.

POST-LESSON CONSIDERATIONS

Post-Instruction Assessment

You will know students are ready to meet the Common Core standard for synthesizing if, in future situations involving the combining of information from two or more sources, students are able to create a common message that combines two or more sources into a single statement.

Links to Common Core Writing Standards

Synthesizing is usually done in order to prepare a written or oral statement about a topic. Consequently, synthesizing is learned best when it is situated in tasks involving the giving of reports, both written and oral. This is reflected in the Common Core writing standards, in which students are expected to *write informational/explanatory texts to examine a topic and convey ideas and information clearly.* Writing such texts typically requires combining information gathered from a variety of sources. Consequently, children learn best when we combine the teaching of synthesizing in reading with writing tasks in which the writer combines information from a variety of sources.

EXAMPLES FOR EXPLAINING
FOUNDATIONAL SKILLS

Example 21

Front–Back/Left–Right/Top–Bottom

(PRINT CONCEPTS—RF STANDARD 1)

BACKGROUND

One of the first things young readers must learn is that certain conventions govern reading. One of the most fundamental of these conventions is the front–back/left–right/top–bottom sequence in which text is read. This system of sequencing text is purely arbitrary; other languages are sequenced in different ways. Because young children often come to school with limited experience with how text is sequenced, they often need this system demonstrated and explained.

> To teach basic features of text such as front–back/left–right/top–bottom, use real text and physically point out the sequence and directionality.

The teaching example provided here is based on the Common Core's kindergarten standard: *RF.K.1a: Follow words from left to right, top to bottom, and page by page.*

> *Note to teachers of other grades:* Hopefully, this basic skill will be fully developed during kindergarten. However, it is not unusual to find students in first grade (and sometimes even in higher grades) who have no experience with how text is sequenced. In those cases, the procedures described here can be applied in much the same form.

PRE-LESSON CONSIDERATIONS

Pre-Instruction Assessment

You will know students are not ready to meet the Common Core standard for print sequencing if, when given a picture book, they do not start at the front and move to the back, do not examine the pages from left to right, and do not move from top to bottom.

Large Conceptual Ideas You Can Reinforce during This Lesson

As you teach this lesson, look for opportunities to reinforce big understandings about reading such as the following:

* What we read has been written by someone.
* Readers can be writers.
* Reading and writing are governed by rules, or conventions, or a code so that we know how to make sense of the squiggles on the page.
* Reading is the key to getting smarter.

ORGANIZING FOR INSTRUCTION

Embedding Instruction in Reading for Purpose and Understanding

It is early in the school year in this kindergarten class, and the teacher is introducing storybooks to the class. Her primary goals are to (1) get students interested in stories, (2) to acquaint them with the idea that books are written by authors, and (3) to get them started on writing simple stories of their own. She chooses to use, over a period of several days, the "Sherlock Chick" stories (by Robert Quackenbush; Parents Magazine Press, 1986). As she reads these stories, she will talk about the author and why he wrote the book, and try to get the students interested in writing their own "Sherlock Chick" books. But she also decides, while doing those things, to also explain and demonstrate how books are sequenced.

Ideas for Differentiating Instruction

One idea you could use if you were this teacher: Because it is early in the school year, the teacher decides to teach this standard to the whole class in a large group. At the end of the lesson, she will do a post-instruction assessment to determine which kindergartners will need additional instruction on print directionality.

THE LESSON

Display, Post, or State the Objective

"By the end of this lesson, you will be able to show me how we read a book from front to back, from left to right, and from top to bottom."

Introducing the Lesson

Say something like:

> "I am going to read some fun books to you. They are written by Robert Quackenbush. While we're reading his books, we will talk about him as an author and we will talk about writing and illustrating your own books. But I am also going to show you how we read books in certain ways."

Stating the Secret to Doing It

Say something like:

> "I'm going to project these books on the white board/smart board, and I'm going to use this laser pointer to show you how we read books in certain ways. You have to pay attention to where we start and in which direction we move."

Modeling the Thinking

Say something like:

> "Today we're going to start with Robert Quackenbush's first book about Sherlock Chick [projects it on the white board/smart board]. It is called *Sherlock Chick's First Case*. Then on other days I will read other Sherlock Chick books to you. Here's the cover of *Sherlock Chick's First Case*. When I start on a book, I begin at the front and move to the back, like this [turns to the next page and uses the laser pointer to reinforce the directionality]. This page is called a

'dedication page.' Robert Quackenbush has dedicated this book to 'Aiden and all the children in Iowa.' Notice the direction of my laser pointer—it moves from the left to the right. We go from the page where the dedication is to the next page, called the title page. Here's the title [points with the laser pointer], and there's a picture of a chicken with a magnifying glass. Now we turn the page again— see how we are going from front to back? When we see lines of print like we see on this page, we move across the print from left to right. Follow my laser pointer while I read [reads, 'The minute their chick was born. . . .']. See how we move from left to right? Now we go to the next line down [points with the laser pointer]. See how we also go from top to bottom? Follow my laser as I read the rest of this page, and as I continue to read the rest of the book. Watch how I go from front to back, from left to right. and from top to bottom."

Scaffolded Assistance

Level 1: Extensive Teacher Help

Say something like:

"Yesterday I read you the first Robert Quackenbush story about Sherlock Chick. Today, I'm going to read you another one [projects on the white board/smart board the book *Sherlock Chick and the Case of the Night Noises*]. This is another fun story by Robert Quackenbush. As we read it, you may be getting some ideas about how you might be able to write your own story about Sherlock Chick. But also remember that we were talking yesterday about the direction in which we go when reading. So we will use the laser pointer again today, but I want you to tell me where I should point it as we read. Where do we start? Yes, at the front. Now where should I point the laser light on the first page? Yes, I should start over here at the left and go to the right. And then where should I go with the light? Yes, we should go down the page."

Level 2: Less Teacher Help

Say something like:

"Yesterday we read a story by Robert Quackenbush. Here's another funny Robert Quackenbush story about Sherlock Chick [projects on the white board/smart board *Sherlock Chick and the Peekaboo Mystery*]. But remember that we are also working on the direction in which we read books. So today I'm going to ask each of you to be the one who uses the laser pointer, so that each of you can show us the direction we move in when we read. Jon, will you be first? Use the pointer to show us where we start reading and how we move across the page."

Level 3: No Teacher Help

Say something like:

> "Today we're going to read another Robert Quackenbush story about Sherlock Chick [projects another story on the white board/smart board]. But today I am not going to use the laser pointer because now you should be able to point to where we start each page and how we move on each page. So each time I show a page, I will have one of you go up and point to where we start and how we move across the page."

Continued Application to Reading

The immediate application of this lesson will occur when students begin creating their own stories about Sherlock Chick. Using invented spelling and their own illustrations, they will make a book, starting at the front and moving to the back, and with print on the page going from left to right and from top to bottom. In subsequent reading situations, of course, the teacher will continue to reinforce the conventions regarding print directionality.

POST-LESSON CONSIDERATIONS

Post-Instruction Assessment

You will know students are ready to meet the Common Core standard for print directionality if, in writing their own books or in reading books, they start at the front and move from left to right and from top to bottom on the page.

Links to Common Core Writing Standards

Print directionality applies to writing as well as reading, and having students engaged in writing, as the above kindergarten teacher does, reinforces learning about how to read text while also meeting the Common Core writing standard *W.K.3: Use a combination of drawing, dictating and writing to narrate a single event or several loosely linked events, tell about the events in the order in which they occurred and provide a reaction to what happened.*

Example 22

Print Detail

(PRINT CONCEPTS—RF STANDARD 1)

BACKGROUND

Recognizing words in print is a visual task. Readers must look at the squiggles on the page and see how they are different. Some children come to school having little experience distinguishing one squiggle from another. They lack the ability to visually discriminate among like forms— that is, they do not attend to the print detail that distinguishes one letter from another or one word from another or one sentence from another.

Print detail is a skill of knowing how to look. For instance, some children look at letters such as *b*, *d*, and *p* and do not "see" how they are different. They do not look different to them because they do not know how to look.

> To teach print detail, focus the student's attention on differences, not similarities. It is the differences that set one letter apart from another. Consequently, when students require assistance in attending to print detail, the explanation focuses on noting differences.

The teaching example provided here is based on the Common Core's first grade standard: *RF.1.1: Demonstrate understanding of the organization and basic features of print.* It assumes a hypothetical first grade.

> *Note for teachers of other grade levels:* The suggestions provided here for teaching print details to first graders can be applied at other grade levels.

For instance, kindergarten teachers would use basically the same explanation when teaching *FS.K.1d: Recognize and name all upper and lowercase letters of the alphabet.* Occasionally, it may even be necessary to teach print details in higher grades, especially if a student is having difficulty remembering words at sight. In such cases, the suggested explanation provided here can be used.

PRE-LESSON CONSIDERATIONS

Pre-Instruction Assessment

You will know students are not ready to meet the Common Core standard for print detail if they say one letter for another (e.g., mix up the letters *d* and *b*) or if they write them incorrectly.

Large Conceptual Understandings You Can Reinforce during This Lesson

As you teach this lesson, look for opportunities to reinforce big understandings about reading such as the following:

- The concepts of "same" and "different."
- Letters are like a code, and in order for the code to be read correctly, the letters always must be made the same way.

ORGANIZING FOR INSTRUCTION

Embedding Instruction in Reading for Purpose and Understanding

In this first grade, the children's project for the day is to learn to follow simple directions when making mud pies. In preparation for doing so, the teacher shares the big book *How to Make a Mud Pie*, by Rozanne Lanczak Williams and Keith Berger (Creative Teaching Press, 1995). But because the teacher has collected assessment data indicating that many of these students do not attend to fine differences in print, she also uses this text as an opportunity to teach print detail.

Ideas for Differentiating Instruction

One idea you could use if you were this teacher: The teacher is teaching this standard to the whole class. However, she will collect post-instruction assessment data at the end. For those students who still need help discriminating print detail, she will do a follow-up lesson in which she will use plastic letters students can manipulate, followed by having them print the easily confused letters on a sand table, stating as they do so how an *m* is different from an *n*.

THE LESSON

Display, Post, or State the Objective

"By the end of this lesson, you will be able to point to the letter *m* and the letter *n*, and you will be able to say how they are different."

Introducing the Lesson

Say something like:

> "We have already talked about the fact that we are going to make mud pies today. In order to do that, we must follow some directions. I'm going to read this big book to you and you will follow along because it describes the steps we must follow to make mud pies. But before we start reading this book, I want to show you how to look closely at letters so you can tell one letter from another. Being able to do that is very important for being able to read books like this big book. What I'm going to show you today is how to tell an *m* from an *n* because there are both *m*'s and *n*'s in the book we are going to read."

Stating the Secret to Doing It

Say something like:

> "The secret to telling an *m* from an *n* is to look at how they are different. They look very much alike, but they are different because one has two humps and the other has only one hump."

Modeling the Thinking

Say something like:

> "Pay close attention to what I do because I will be asking you to tell *m*'s from *n*'s when we read our book about mud pies. I am writing an *m* and an *n* on the board. In order to tell these letters apart, we must use our eyes and look for differences between them. When I look at this letter [points to the *m*], I see two humps. This is the *m*. The *m* has two humps. I'm going to put a little *x* over each hump. When I look at this letter [points to the *n*], I see only one hump. This is the *n*. I can tell it's an *n* because it only has one hump. So I put a little *x* over that one to help me remember that it is an *n*. The *m* and *n* look very much alike because they both have humps. But they are not exactly the same. The *m* has two humps, but the *n* only has one hump. So I can tell them apart because they have a different number of humps."

Scaffolded Assistance

Level 1: Extensive Teacher Help

Say something like:

> "Let's see if you can tell *m*'s from *n*'s and tell me why they're different. I will give you lots of help this time by leaving my little *x*'s on the humps. When I point to a letter, count the number of humps and tell me whether it is an *m* or an *n*, and tell me how you know which is which."

Level 2: Less Teacher Help

Say something like:

> "Now I'm going to make it harder. Let's see if you can tell which is an *m* and which is an *n* if I remove the little *x*'s. Now when I point to a letter, you must tell me which it is and how you know, but you won't have the little *x*'s to help you."

Level 3: No Teacher Help

Once students have demonstrated the ability to distinguish one letter from the other, have them identify *m*'s and *n*'s in *How to Make a Mud Pie*. Read the book to students first for information about how to make mud pies, but then return to the text to have them identify *m*'s and *n*'s.

Continued Application to Reading

This example illustrates how a skill can be taught before applying it in a book. The skill of discriminating print detail is applied in the book on mud pies today, but the teacher will also look for other opportunities on subsequent days to apply what has been learned to other texts.

POST-LESSON CONSIDERATIONS

Post-Instruction Assessment

You will know students are ready to meet the Common Core standard for print detail when you note that students no longer mix up letters when identifying them and/or no longer form them incorrectly in their writing.

Links to Common Core Writing Standards

The more students write letters, the faster and more accurately they will discriminate one letter from another in print. Consequently, the more often we engage students in writing letter forms, the better they will be at "reading" them.

Example 23

Discriminating among Sounds

(PHONOLOGICAL AWARENESS—RF STANDARD 2)

BACKGROUND

Phonological awareness is the ability to distinguish among sounds. It is a crucial prerequisite to phonics because you cannot use letters to figure out an unknown word if you cannot tell one letter sound from another. It is an auditory skill. The goal is for students to hear the differences in sounds. Consequently, students use only their ears.

Phonological awareness is a prereading skill and is most often taught to emergent readers. However, some children come to school already knowing how to discriminate among sounds because they have played sound games at home, have sung rhyming songs, have had stories read to them containing funny sounds, and have engaged in other activities involving discrimination among sounds.

Children who have not had such experience prior to school, however, will need to develop phonological awareness skills. This involves being able to match rhyming words, being able to tell when words end or begin with the same sound, being able to segment words into separate sounds, and being able to blend sounds together.

> To teach phonological awareness, separate and exaggerate the sounds. Do not tie the sounds to letter names. The focus here is on discriminating sounds, not naming letters that make the sound.

The example provided here is based on the Common Core standard *RF.K.2d: Isolate and pronounce the initial, medial vowel, and final sounds (phonemes).* It assumes a hypothetical kindergarten classroom.

204

Note to teachers of other grade levels: While phonological awareness is most frequently taught in kindergarten, it is not unusual for older children to need instruction in discriminating sounds. In such cases, the explanation provided here, and the emphasis on exaggerating sounds, can be used in much the same way when helping older students.

PRE-LESSON CONSIDERATIONS

Pre-Instruction Assessment

You will know students are not ready to meet this particular Common Core standard for phonological awareness if they cannot tell whether the words you say have the same or different sound at the beginning.

Large Conceptual Ideas You Can Reinforce during This Lesson

As you teach this lesson, look for opportunities to reinforce big understandings about reading such as the following:

- Being able to distinguish among sounds is a crucial prerequisite to learning phonics.
- One must know the meaning of the words *beginning, end, same,* and *different.*

ORGANIZING FOR INSTRUCTION

Embedding Instruction in Reading for Purpose and Understanding

This example is set in a kindergarten class. During "show-and-tell," one of the students reported seeing a television program the night before about migrating whales. The student's report resulted in a lively discussion of whales. The teacher decided to use the discussion of whales as a "teachable moment" for developing with five of the students the Common Core standard for discriminating whether words begin with the same sound or different sounds. She uses her *Big Book Magazine* on whales (Issue Number 1, Scholastic, 1989).

> ### Ideas for Differentiating Instruction
>
> *One idea you could use if you were this teacher:* Students who are not working with you on this standard go to interest centers around the classroom where they can independently use the audio tapes, computers, and/or picture books that are available there.

THE LESSON

Display, Post, or State the Objective

"By the end of this lesson, you will be able to tell whether a word I say begins with the same sound or a different sound, and you will be able to say the sound at the beginning."

Introducing the Lesson

Say something like:

> "All our talk about whales reminds me of one of my favorite poems. It is on the front page of this *Big Book Magazine* about whales. Listen while I read this poem to you, and try to figure out what the author of the poem is saying about the whale's tail. After we discuss the poem, we will listen to some of the words the poet uses and decide whether they sound the same or different at the beginning."

Stating the Secret to Doing It

Say something like:

> "The secret to being able to do this is to use only your ears and to separate the beginning sound from the ending sound of the word. We are only concerned with the sound. We will not be naming the letter that makes the sound."

Modeling the Thinking

Say something like:

> "Now that we've finished discussing this poem about whales, I want to show you how to tell whether words sound the same or different

at the beginning. This is an important skill to learn if you are going to be able to read books like this yourselves. Listen carefully to what I do so you, too, can listen to words and tell whether they sound the same or different at the beginning.

"In order to tell whether a word is the same or different at the beginning, we must say the word slowly and separate the beginning sound from the rest of the word. For instance, in our poem about a whale, we had the words *whale* and *snail*. They sound very much alike. But I'll say each word slowly: *whhhh—ale . . . snnn—ail*. By stretching out the word and separating out the beginning sound, I can tell that whale begins with a *whhh* sound and that *snail* begins with a *snnnn* sound. So I know they are different at the beginning because one begins with the *whhhh* sound and the other begins with the *snnn* sound."

Scaffolded Assistance

Level 1: Extensive Teacher Help

Say something like:

> "Here are two other words from the poem. One is *tail* and the other is the word we used before—*whale*. I'm going to help you this time by separating the beginning sound in each word for you. You listen and tell me if the words are the same or different at the beginning. *Ttttt—ail. . . .Whhh—ale*. What sound do you hear at the beginning of *ttt*—ail? Yes, the sound is *t-t-t* at the beginning. What sound do you hear at the beginning of *whhhh—ale*? Yes, the sound is *whhhh* at the beginning. So do these words sound the same or different at the beginning? How do you know?"

Level 2: Less Teacher Help

Say something like:

> "Now let's try it with two other words that were in the poem: *that* and *there*. This time I'm not going to help you by stretching out the sounds for you. You will have to separate the beginning sound from the ending yourselves. Let's see you try it with the word *that*. Now stretch out the word *there*. What sound do you hear at the beginning

of *that?* What sound did you hear at the beginning of *there?* Is the sound the same or different?"

Level 3: No Teacher Help

Say something like:

> "Now let's try listening to words in another story in my *Big Book Magazine*. This is the story of "Humphrey, the Wrong Way Whale." I'm going to read the story; then we will go back and listen to some of the words in the story, such as *wrong* and *way* and *whale*, to decide whether they begin with the same sound or with different sounds."

Continued Application to Reading

Ultimately, the ability to discriminate among sounds will be applied in the learning of phonics (in tasks such as are illustrated in Examples 24 and 25). In the meantime, however, the teacher will give students opportunities to discriminate among sounds in stories she shares with them.

POST-LESSON CONSIDERATIONS

Post-Instruction Assessment

You will know students will be ready to meet the standard for this particular kind of phonological awareness if they are able to say whether two words sound the same or different at the beginning and are able to say the sound they hear at the beginning.

Links to Common Core Writing Standards

Students who need instruction in phonological awareness are typically writing only squiggle marks on the page or using beginning forms of invented spelling and are not yet ready to meet Common Core writing standards. Nonetheless, students will be labeling pictures with their invented words. On those occasions, student can be asked whether certain pairs of words they invented begin with the same or different sounds.

Example 24

Letter–Sound Association
(PHONICS AND WORD RECOGNITION—
RF STANDARD 3)

BACKGROUND

Phonics instruction begins by tying particular consonant letters to the sounds they typically make. Phonological awareness is a prerequisite. But unlike phonological awareness, students must pay attention to both the visual form of the letter and the sound it makes.

To teach letter–sound associations, ensure that students are looking at the letter as they are saying the sound of the letter.

The teaching example provided here is based on the Common Core standard *RF.K.3a: Demonstrate basic knowledge of one-to-one letter–sound correspondences by producing the primary sound or many of the most frequent sounds for each consonant.* It assumes a hypothetical kindergarten classroom.

Note for teachers of other grade levels: It is not unusual to find students at higher grade levels who do not know the sounds certain consonant letters make. When that happens, the suggestions provided here can be applied. Regardless of grade level, the instructional focus should be on looking at the letter (or letter combination) at the same time you say the sound.

PRE-LESSON CONSIDERATIONS

Pre-Instruction Assessment

You will know students are not ready to meet the Common Core standard for letter–sound correspondences if, when they encounter a new word having the particular consonant letter in the initial position, they do not attempt to say the first sound, or they say the sound incorrectly.

Large Conceptual Ideas You Can Reinforce during This Lesson

During this lesson, look for opportunities to reinforce big understandings about reading such as:

- Reading is talk written down.
- Alphabet letters are a code standing for the sounds we make when we talk.
- Different letters make different sounds but sometimes a single letter will make more than one sound.

ORGANIZING FOR INSTRUCTION

Embedding Instruction in Reading for Purpose and Understanding

This example assumes a kindergarten class involved in making their own picture books about animals. They will "read" their books to friends in the school's other kindergarten class. During the project, the teacher supports students' efforts to write animal books by reading various animal stories to the class. Some of the students have already met the standard for the letter sound *s*, but a group of seven students have not. For that group, the teacher uses another animal book—the big book *Who Is the Beast?* by Keith Baker (Harcourt Brace Jovanovich, 1990) because it has several words that begin with the letter *s*.

Ideas for Differentiating Instruction

One idea you could use if you were this teacher: Students not working with you on this standard continue working at their desks making the picture books about animals that they will be reading to the other kindergarten class.

THE LESSON

Display, Post, or State the Objective

"By the end of this lesson, you will be able to say the sound of the letter s when you find the letter s at the beginning of a word you don't know."

Introducing the Lesson

Say something like:

> "As part of our writing project on animals, I am going to read this big book to you [holds up *Who Is the Beast?*]. It's a wonderful story with an interesting message. It may give you some ideas you can use when you are writing your own animal stories. But before we begin, I want to teach you a new letter sound because there are several words in this story that begin with this sound. I'm going to teach you the sound the letter s makes at the beginning of many words."

Stating the Secret to Doing It

Say something like:

> "The secret to learning the sound the letter s makes at the beginning of a word is to say the letter sound at the same time you point to the letter s."

Modeling the Thinking

Say something like:

> "Pay attention to how I learn this letter sound. First, I look at this word [writes *say* on the board]. It begins with the letter s. To learn the sound s makes here, I point to the letter as I stretch out the sound. It is saying the s-s-s-s-s sound, so I say that sound while pointing to the letter s. To remember the letter sound, I look at the letter at the same time I say the sound."

Scaffolded Assistance

Level 1: Extensive Teacher Help

Say something like:

> "Here's a new word that begins with s [points to the word *sound*]. It is one of the s words we will find in our story today. Let's work together on this one so I can help you. Point to the letter *s* and, together with me, say the *s-s-s* sound. Ready? Look and say *s-s-s*."

Level 2: Less Teacher Help

Say something like:

> "Okay, this time I'm not going to give you so much help. You have to say the sound yourself instead of doing it in unison with me. Here's another word beginning with *s* [points to the word *sight*]. First, point to the letter *s*. Good. Now, while you are pointing to the letter, say the sound the *s* makes. Good. It makes the *s-s-s* sound."

Level 3: No Teacher Help

Say something like:

> "Here are two more words beginning with *s* that appear in our story [writes the words *so* and *side* on the board]. Look at these words and say the sound the first letter makes."

> Note: Be sure to use only words that make the /s/ sound. For instance, the word *sure* also appears in the story, but we would not use it because it makes a *sh-sh-sh* sound, not the *s-s-s* sound.

Continued Application to Reading

In subsequent books the teacher reads to the class, she will continue to point out words beginning with the letter *s* and ask students to provide the sound at the beginning of that word.

POST-LESSON CONSIDERATIONS

Post-Instruction Assessment

You will know students are ready to meet the Common Core standard for letter–sound correspondences if students say the correct sound when they encounter new words beginning with that letter sound.

Links to Common Core Writing Standards

The writing activity the kindergartners are doing in this example is consistent with the Common Core writing standard *W.K.2: Use a combination of drawing, dictating, and writing to compose informative/explanatory texts in which they name what they are writing about and supply some information about the topic.*

Using words beginning with *s* in their writing also illustrates the application of this standard to spelling. Once a letter–sound association is established in reading, students can then use it to spell words that begin with that sound. For instance, the kindergartners in this example would be able to spell the first letter of words beginning with *s* when writing their animal stories.

Example 25

Vowel Patterns
(PHONICS AND WORD RECOGNITION—
RF STANDARD 3)

BACKGROUND

Letter–sound correspondences are harder to learn with vowels than with consonants because vowels can make many different sounds. Consequently, it is easier to learn vowel sounds by looking for patterns in which the reader figures out unknown words by chunks rather than letter-by-letter. For instance, a student who knows the word *each* as a sight word can figure out the unknown word *peach* if he also knows the sound of the consonant *p*.

This strategy is sometimes known as "decoding by analogy" because the unknown word is figured out by comparing it to a known word. It is also sometimes referred to as an "onset rime" in which the "onset" is the beginning consonant and the "rime" is the known spelling pattern.

While it is possible to sound out individual vowels in an unknown word rather than chunking with vowel patterns, it is a laborious process. Few students become proficient at it because of the numerous variations in vowel sounds. Using vowel patterns minimizes the vowel problem because the known spelling pattern, or rime, includes the vowel sound. Given the known phonogram pattern, students can substitute consonants into the initial or final position. For instance, if a student knows the word *man*, he can figure out the word *pan* and also the word *map*.

> To teach vowel patterns, begin with a known sight word having a common vowel pattern and then teach students to substitute different consonants in the initial or final positions.

The teaching example provided here is based on the Common Core second-grade standard *R.F.2.3a: Distinguish long and short vowels when reading regularly spelled one-syllable words.* It assumes a hypothetical second-grade classroom.

> *Note for teachers of other grade levels:* It is not unusual to find students in grade 4 or higher who have difficulty with vowel sounds. In those cases, the suggestions provided here are equally applicable. The focus remains on the common phonogram pattern (or rime) and on substituting consonants (or onsets) into that pattern.

PRE-LESSON CONSIDERATIONS

Pre-Instruction Assessment

You will know students are not ready to meet the Common Core standard for using vowel sounds if, when they are reading text, they are unable to say one-syllable words that contain common spelling patterns.

Large Conceptual Ideas You Can Reinforce during This Lesson

As you teach this lesson, look for opportunities to reinforce big understandings about reading such as the following:

• Words often are made up of common spelling patterns.
• It is more efficient to decode unknown words in chunks rather than doing it letter-by-letter.
• Phonics is an important strategy when we meet unknown words; however, we want to know most words at sight so we can read fluently.

ORGANIZING FOR INSTRUCTION

Embedding Instruction in Reading for Purpose and Understanding

This example assumes a second-grade class involved in a poetry writing project, with the intent of displaying their poems in a schoolwide literacy display. As part of the project, the teacher shares poetry with the class daily. Today she will read poems from Shel Silverstein's *A Light in the Attic* (Harper & Row, 1981). However, because several students in the class have not yet met the standard for vowels, she gathers those students together for instruction. She uses Silverstein's poem "The Dragon of Grindly Grun" to teach these students how to figure out words having common vowel patterns.

Ideas for Differentiating Instruction

One idea you could use if you were this teacher: Students not working with you on this standard have been directed to the website *www. poetryarchive.org* where they can read poems written by other children. They select a favorite poem and practice reading it aloud to a partner for later presentation to the class.

THE LESSON

Display, Post, or State the Objective

"By the end of this lesson, you will be able to figure out unknown words in the poem we are going to read together by using common spelling patterns of words we know at sight."

Introducing the Lesson

Say something like:

> "We're going to read a funny poem by Shel Silverstein today. But it has some hard words in it so I am going to first show you how to figure out those hard words."

Stating the Secret to Doing It

Say something like:

> "The secret to figuring out these hard words is to look first to see if the unknown word has a familiar spelling pattern or rime and to substitute the beginning sound into the rime."

Modeling the Thinking

Say something like:

> "Let me show you how I do it. Let's say I'm reading along and I run into the word *fun*. If I don't know that word, I have to stop and figure it out. I know the sound of the letter *f* so I can make the beginning sound. But I don't know how to say the rest of the word because I don't know what sound the vowel is making. So I look at the *-un* in the word and ask myself, 'Do I know a sight word that ends with the letters *-un*?' Yes, I know the word *run*. So I take off the *r* in *run* and put an *f* in its place. Now I say the sound of *f* and the *-un*, and I end up with the word *fun*. So what you do to figure out words where you know the initial sound but don't know the rest of the word is to look for a rime or spelling pattern in the word that is the same as the spelling pattern of a word you know by sight, then take off the first letter, put on the first letter of the new word, and say the rest of the word."

Scaffolded Assistance

Level 1: Extensive Teacher Help

Say something like:

> "I'm going to show you some words that are like the new words we will be seeing in the Shel Silverstein poem we read today. For each of the new words, I have underlined the spelling pattern that is the same as *run* to help you separate the beginning sound from the rime. What I want you to do is to figure out how to say these words and to tell me how you figured out how to say them. The first word is *spun*."

Level 2: Less Teacher Help

Say something like:

> "Here are some more words that are like the new words we will see in the poem we read today. But I am making it harder this time because I have not underlined the spelling pattern. You have to figure out the spelling pattern yourself and think about how you are going to figure out the word. The first word is *stun*."

Level 3: No Teacher Help

Say something like:

> "I have written out some sentences on cards. Each of these sentences has a new word in it that used the spelling pattern we are working on. What you need to do is read the sentence and, when you come to the new word, figure it out using our new strategy."

Continued Application to Reading

Once students are able to use the spelling pattern in a scaffolded situation, they read the Silverstein poem and apply their strategy as they are reading. In subsequent reading of poems and stories, the teacher reminds students to apply the strategy if they encounter words where they know the initial consonant sound but don't know how to say the rest of the word.

POST-LESSON CONSIDERATIONS

Post-Instruction Assessment

You will know students are ready to meet the Common Core standard for vowel sounds if, when they encounter unknown words having a familiar spelling pattern, they figure out the word by substituting the initial consonant of the unknown word and combining it with the common spelling pattern.

Links to Common Core Writing Standards

The students' engagement in writing of poetry is consistent with the Common Core's writing standard about writing of narratives (RF.W.2.3). Additionally, once students are using this strategy to figure out unknown words encountered in print, they can be encouraged to use the same strategy when spelling. The process is much the same in that the student listens to the sound of the word being spelled, thinks of a known word having that sound, and uses the ending of the known word to spell the new word.

Example 26

Syllabication

(PHONICS AND WORD RECOGNITION—
RF STANDARD 3)

BACKGROUND

Decoding multisyllable words is difficult. Part of what makes syllabication difficult, of course, is that the words are long. But it is also difficult because many long words have vowel combinations unfamiliar to young readers. Consider, for instance, the word *syllable:* neither the *syl-* at the beginning nor the *-ble* at the end is a commonly encountered phonic pattern in early reading. It's not that these vowel patterns are irregular (*y* sometimes acts as a vowel, and the consonant plus *le* at the end appears in a number of words). However, these vowel combinations only appear occasionally, are not routine and, therefore, are more difficult.

The only real consistency in syllabication is that every syllable must have a vowel sound. However, that doesn't mean every syllable will have a single vowel letter. To the contrary, many syllables, while having only one vowel sound, have more than one vowel letter.

Consequently, if you know what the word is and can say it, it is relatively easy to break it into syllables. You simply say the word slowly, emphasizing the vowel sounds and then identify the syllables. You stretch out the word, saying, "syyyl – aaaa – ble." There are three vowel sounds, so there are three syllables.

But this is not what readers do. A reader's task is not to identify the number of syllables; rather, it is to figure out how to say the word she doesn't know on the page. If *syllable* is an unknown word encountered in a text, and the student has not yet had much experience with *y* as a vowel or with the consonant plus *le* ending, it will be a difficult word to sound out.

Consequently, there are many limitations to using syllabication to figure out unknown words. In addition to knowing that every syllable must have a vowel sound, students must apply what they have previously learned about vowel patterns (see Example 25) and what they have previously learned about using context to figure out unknown words (see Example 14).

> To teach syllabication, ensure that students know that every syllable has a vowel sound. Then have them examine the word for vowels and/or vowel patterns, make a trial pronunciation for each pattern using what they have learned about vowel patterns, and then combine the trial pronunciation with context clues from the text and try to predict what the unknown word is.

The teaching example provided here is based on the Common Core standard for third grade (*RF.3.3c: Decode multi-syllable words*). It assumes a hypothetical third-grade classroom.

> *Note for teachers of other grades:* As soon as young readers encounter longer words in their reading, they will need to know how to break them into syllables as a means of identifying them. The recommendations provided here regarding examining words for vowel patterns and then using context clues can be used when teaching syllabication at any grade level. The focus on vowels, on vowel patterns, and on using context to confirm whether a pronunciation was correct does not change from one grade to another.

PRE-LESSON CONSIDERATIONS

Pre-Instruction Assessment

You will know students are not ready to meet the Common Core standard for syllabication when, during the reading of text, students stop when a multisyllable word is encountered and make no attempt to sound it out.

Large Conceptual Idea You Can Reinforce during This Lesson

As you teach this lesson, look for opportunities to reinforce big understandings about reading such as the following:

- Reading and writing empowers us to be able to do useful things.
- Readers have to be proactive and tentative both in comprehending text and in trying to figure out long unknown words.

ORGANIZING FOR INSTRUCTION

Embedding Instruction in Reading for Purpose and Understanding

In this third-grade classroom, the teacher and students have decided to publish a monthly newspaper that will be distributed to the other classes in the building. In preparing to become publishers and reporters, they have been reading informational text about newspapers. In doing so, they have encountered unknown words such as *publisher, editorial, circulation,* and *advertising.* Some of the better readers in the class have no difficulty identifying these words, but others who have not yet met the standard for syllabication cannot figure out what these words are. For those students, the teacher decides to do a lesson on how to syllabicate such hard words and uses the website *www.kidscoop.com,* an Internet news site that supplies news items for student newspapers, as the text for the lesson.

Ideas for Differentiating Instruction

One idea you could use if you were this teacher: Students who are not working with you on this standard select independent activities from among several centers around the room. At each center, there is a set of directions and all necessary materials for pursuing tasks associated with putting a newspaper together.

THE LESSON

Display, Post, or State the Objective

"By the end of this lesson, you will be able to pronounce the long hard words you have been encountering in your reading of newspapers."

Introducing the Lesson

Say something like:

> "Yesterday we ran into some really long, hard words in our reading about newspapers. So today I am going to show you how to sound out those hard words. We'll start with this text from the 'kidscoop' website [displays the page on her white board/smart board]. But when we are done with that, we should be able to go back to the hard words we ran into yesterday and figure those words out."

Stating the Secret to Doing It

Say something like:

> "The secret to being able to say long hard words is to break the word into smaller parts, called syllables. Each syllable has a vowel sound. So what we do is look at the long word to see where the vowels are, say each vowel section using what you know about vowel patterns, then say the whole word together, and finally look at the context of the text to see if what you said makes sense in that place."

Modeling the Thinking

Say something like:

> "Let me show you how to do it using this page from the 'kidscoop' website. Let's say I don't know this word [points to the word *content*]. To try to figure it out, I first look for vowels because I know each part of a long word has a vowel sound. I see the vowel *o* in the first part of the word and I see the vowel *e* in the last part. Using what I know about vowel patterns, I can take the *-on*, add the *c* to the beginning, and say 'con.' Then at the end of the word I can take the *-en* and put a *t* on at the beginning, add a *t* at the end, and say 'tent.' When I put them together, I say 'con-tent.' Then I have to see if it makes sense in the sentence on the page. It says, '. . . award-winning *content* for your newspaper.' Oh, that makes sense. The word is *content*."

Scaffolded Assistance

Level 1: Extensive Teacher Help

Say something like:

> "Okay, now let's see if you can help me do one. Here's a hard word [points to the word *family*]. If I don't know this word, I will try to sound it out in parts, or syllables. What do we do first? Yes, look for the vowels or vowel patterns. How many vowels do we see? Yes, there are three. So we can expect that there will be three syllables. Let's look at the first one. If you use what you have learned about vowel patterns, what could you say that first sound is? Okay, now look at the second vowel. What might that say? Now look at the *y*, which acts as a vowel in this word. Now put the first sound and the second sound and the third sound together. What do you get? Okay. It still doesn't sound like a word we know? Okay, let's look at the context and see if that will help us. The sentence says, '. . . kids and their *family*.' Does that help? Yes, the word is *family*."

Level 2: Less Teacher Help

Say something like:

> "Let's try another word, but this time you must do more of the work. Here's a hard word on the 'kidscoop' page [points to the word *selections*]. What will we do first? Yes, look at the vowels or vowel patterns. How many are there? So, if there are three vowels or vowel patterns, how many syllables will the word have? Yes, three, so now try to say each syllable, using what you know about vowel patterns to help you. Okay, now try to put the three sounds together. Yes, it still doesn't sound right, does it? So let's look at the context for help. Yes, when you put it in the sentence '. . . reading *selections* and games . . .' it makes sense. The word is *selection*."

Level 3: No Teacher Help

The next word the teacher points to on the "kidscoop" page is the word *sample*. She gives no help in figuring out this word other than offering questions at each point along the way.

Continued Application to Reading

Once students have demonstrated ability to sound out multisyllable words on the "kidscoop" page, the students move to the words *publisher, editorial, circulation,* and *advertising.* As students continue their work on the newspaper, as well as when they are doing other reading, the teacher will remind them of how to figure out the long words they encounter.

POST-LESSON CONSIDERATIONS

Post-Instruction Assessment

You will know students are ready to meet the Common Core standard for syllabication if, when they encounter an unknown multisyllable word in their reading, they pause, identify the syllables, and use context to make a final determination of what the word is.

Links to Common Core Writing Standards

The major link to writing is spelling. When writing a text and faced with spelling a long word, students can use what they know about syllabication. They would say the word, listen for the vowel sounds, and spell the word using the vowel sounds they hear.

Example 27

Sight-Word Recognition
(PHONICS AND WORD RECOGNITION— RF STANDARD 3)

BACKGROUND

All good readers instantly recognize and name most of the words they encounter in print. That is, they recognize the words "at sight."

Recognizing words "at sight" is important from the earliest stages of reading. Emergent readers, for instance, must instantly recognize such common words as *the, come, have, do,* and *here,* all of which are spelled irregularly (i.e., none of them can be figured out using phonic rules).

While phonics receives much of our instructional emphasis, what we ultimately want is for students to recognize most words at sight. For instance, the generally accepted standard for placing students in "just-right" reading material is their ability to recognize at sight 90–95% of the words on the page.

The first goal in sight-word instruction is to help students recognize the 300 or so most common words in the English language. Many of these are irregularly spelled words.

But in the long run the goal is to develop the understanding that good readers know by sight all the words they are likely to encounter in routine, daily reading. Good instruction in sight-word recognition, therefore, results not only in acquisition of a stock of instantly recognized words but also in an understanding that the ultimate goal is to recognize virtually all words at sight.

The best way for students to accumulate a large stock of sight words is to ensure that they do lots and lots of reading of easy books. In the early stages, repeatedly reading favorite books helps students instantly recognize the words in that book. But when reading more difficult books, and especially when reading informational text in content areas such as social studies and science, students often need teachers to directly teach both the word meaning (see Example 13) and how to instantly recognize the word (this example).

> To teach students to instantly recognize words, point out the visually distinctive features of the word and then ensure lots of repetition in which the student looks at the word while saying its name.

The example provided here is based on the Common Core standard *RF.1.1g: Recognize and read grade-appropriate irregularly spelled words.* It assumes a hypothetical first-grade classroom.

> *Note to teachers of other grade levels:* This example is set in a first grade, but it is often necessary in higher grades to teach students to instantly recognize words at sight. In those instances, instruction remains the same. The suggestions provided here regarding the importance both of attending to the visual form of the word and of repetition apply when teaching sight-word recognition at all grade levels.

PRE-LESSON CONSIDERATIONS

Pre-Instruction Assessment

You will know students are not ready to meet the Common Core standard for recognizing and reading unknown words if students pause for extended periods when encountering words or say the words incorrectly.

Large Conceptual Ideas You Can Reinforce during This Lesson

As you teach this lesson, look for opportunities to reinforce big understandings about reading such as the following:

- Good readers recognize most words instantly.
- Sight-word recognition is a task of "looking and saying"; it is not a task of sounding out a word.
- The ultimate goal in word identification is to know as many words as possible at sight because when you know all the words reading is a lot more fun.

ORGANIZING FOR INSTRUCTION

Embedding Instruction in Reading for Purpose and Understanding

This example is set in a first-grade class in which the students are doing a project involving the production of a book for the classroom library entitled *How Different Animals Are Different.* They will dictate the text to the teacher and will draw the illustrations themselves. In pursuit of this topic, the teacher is planning to share the book *Legs, Legs, Legs,* by Carol Krueger (Lands End Publishing, 1993). It is an informational text that distinguishes among various animals by the number of legs they have. Students will be able to use the information in writing their own books about how animals are different. But the irregularly spelled word *come* appears several times in the text, and the teacher knows from earlier assessments that several students cannot recognize the word at sight. Consequently, before beginning the reading of the *Legs, Legs, Legs* book, the teacher gathers these several students together to teach them the sight word *come.*

Ideas for Differentiating Instruction

One idea you could use if you were this teacher: Students not working with you on this standard have been given a variety of tasks to complete. They are tiered in difficulty according to students' reading levels, but all involve the gathering of information for use in their project on how animals are different.

THE LESSON

Display, Post, or State the Objective

"By the end of this lesson, you will be able to recognize and say the word *come* instantly every time you see it in the animal book we are going to read together today."

Introducing the Lesson

Say something like:

> "We have been reading about animals in order to write our own book for the classroom library, and we have been learning lots of

new words. We have also been learning that good readers remember these words and say them instantly whenever they see them in a book or in writing. Today we are going to read a book together. This book will give us lots of information about how animals are different, so we will be able to use that information when we write our own book. But this book also uses a new word we will be seeing often. So before we start reading the book, let's learn this new word."

Stating the Secret to Doing It

Say something like:

> "The secret to remembering new words is to pay close attention to what it looks like, especially at the beginning and the end, and then we will need to point to the word and say its name several times while we're looking at it."

Modeling the Thinking

Say something like:

> "The new word we are going to learn is *come*. I am writing it here on the board. Let me show you how I remember words like this. I can't use my phonics skills because this word doesn't follow the rules. So I have to look closely at the letters in the word, paying special attention to the first and last letters. When I look at the beginning I see the letter *c*. I close my eyes and picture the beginning letter in my mind. Then I look at the ending. I see the letter *e*. So I close my eyes and picture both the beginning and the ending letters. I'm trying to hold a picture of the word in my mind. Then, with my eyes still closed, I use my finger to write on the rug in front of me the letters I see in my mind while saying the word. Then I look at the board and see if what I wrote with my finger looks the same as the word on the board. I do that several times until I can write and say the word correctly every time."

Scaffolded Assistance

Level 1: Extensive Teacher Help

Say something like:

> "Let's see if you can do as I did. Look carefully at the word I have written on the board. Now close your eyes. What do you see as the first letter in the word? Okay. Now look at the word again, close your eyes, and picture both the beginning letter and the ending letter. Good. Now use your finger to trace the letters in the word on the rug in front of you as you say the word out loud."

Level 2: Less Teacher Help

Say something like:

> "I have two index cards here. On one I have printed the word *come*, and on the other I have printed the same letters but I have mixed them up. The second card does not say *come* because the letters are not in the right order. I'm going to show you each card for just a second or so because what we are trying to learn is to recognize the word *come* instantly. If the card I show you has the word *come* on it, say 'come.' If the card I show you does not have the letters in the right order, don't say anything. We'll do this several times to give you practice looking at and saying the word when it is written correctly. "

Level 3: No Teacher Help

Once students are recognizing the word correctly, the teacher can use the index card with *come* correctly spelled as a flash card. She will insert the *come* card into a pile with other words the students have previously learned at sight, and then she will flash the cards to students. Students must say the word instantly when it is flashed.

Continued Application to Reading

The immediate application will occur as the class and the teacher read *Leg, Legs, Legs*. Each student will have an opportunity to point to and name the word *come* when it appears in the text. Subsequently, the teacher will ensure that students encounter the word *come* in text they read on other occasions, and will continue to remind students that it is a word they should say instantly.

POST-LESSON CONSIDERATIONS

Post-Instruction Assessment

You will know students are ready to meet the Common Core standard for instantly recognizing and saying words if, during the reading of real text, they say the word instantly and correctly.

Links to Common Core Writing Standards

The Common Core specifies that first graders should be writing informational and explanatory text, and the book the students in this first grade are composing is an example of this standard. In addition, having students use the words being taught as sight words in the writing they do will increase the likelihood of the word being recognized in print in the future.

Example 28

Structural Analysis

(PHONICS AND WORD RECOGNITION— RF STANDARD 3)

BACKGROUND

Another way to figure out unknown words is through meaning units, which linguists call "morphemic analysis." The Common Core uses the term *morphology*; reading teachers often use the term *structural analysis*.

There are four kinds of structural units, or morphemes or meaning units, students can use to figure out unknown words:

1. The compound word *snowman* is made up of two morphemes or meaning units—*snow* and *man*.
2. Prefixes and suffixes (or what the Common Core calls "roots and affixes") are meaning units (e.g., the prefix *un-* in *unhappy* means "not," and the suffix *-ful* in *joyful* means "full" as in "full of joy").
3. Inflectional endings such as the plural -s and the ending -ed are morphemes that signal meaning (the plural -s means more than one, and the ending -ed means something happened in the past).
4. Older students often learn to use Greek and Latin roots to identify words.

When students know about morphology, they can use it as a quick and easy way to identify words. However, using morphology only works when the unknown word contains a structural unit.

To teach structural units, focus students' attention on the known root word, have them say that, then have them add the structural unit (e.g., prefix, inflectional ending, etc.).

The teaching example provided here uses compound words to illustrate how to teach Common Core standards such as *RF.1.3f: inflectional endings, RF.2.3d: common prefixes and suffixes,* and *RF.3.3a: common Latin suffixes.* It assumes a hypothetical first-grade classroom.

Note to teachers of other grade levels: While the Common Core does not specify a standard for compound words, the instructional suggestions provided here can be applied in much the same way when teaching inflectional endings, prefixes and suffixes, and Latin and Greek roots.

PRE-LESSON CONSIDERATIONS

Pre-Instruction Assessment

You will know students are not ready to meet the Common Core standard for morphology if, when encountering an unknown word containing a structural unit, they cannot say the word.

Large Understandings You Can Reinforce during This Lesson

As you teach this lesson, look for opportunities to reinforce big understandings about reading such as:

- Words can be made up of a combination of two or more structural units (such as compounds, prefixes, etc.).
- Using structural units to figure out unknown words works only when the unknown word contains structural units.

ORGANIZING FOR INSTRUCTION

Embedding Instruction in Reading for Purpose and Understanding

This lesson is being taught to a first-grade class working on an ecology unit in which the end goal is to produce an exhibit for the school's science fair. Because these first graders are just beginning to read, the teacher is guiding their reading of *The Sea Otter,* by Maggie Blake (Wright Group, 1996). The primary reason for reading this informational text is to gain information for use in creating the science fair exhibit. However, because the students have not yet learned to figure out unknown words using structural units (morphology), and because the text contains many compound words such as *shellfish, fishermen, seaweed, waterproof, underwater,* and *playground,* the teacher decides to explain how to figure out compound words as a first step in teaching the use of morphology.

Ideas for Differentiating Instruction

One idea you could use if you were this teacher: Because the technique of figuring out words using structural units is new, almost everyone in the class needs instruction. Consequently, this example occurs in a whole-class setting. The teacher will attend closely to the post-instruction assessment in anticipation that, following this lesson, there will be a few students who will need additional help.

THE LESSON

Display, Post, or State the Objective

"By the end of this lesson, you will be able to use structural units to figure out words called 'compound words' that appear in today's book on sea otters."

Introducing the Lesson

Say something like:

> "As part of our ecology project for the science fair, we are reading *The Sea Otter* to find out how otters relate to other creatures in the world. But when we read this book together, we are going to find some hard words that we don't know. So, before we start, I want to teach you how to figure out these words. They are called 'compound words' because they are made up of two words."

Stating the Secret to Doing It

Say something like:

> "The secret to figuring out an unknown word that is a 'compound word' is to find the two smaller words you know in it and then combine those words into a single word."

Modeling the Thinking

Say something like:

> "Watch me while I show you how I figure out unknown words that are compounds. Let's look at this sentence I'm writing on the board [writes 'I made a big snowman on the playground today']. When I am reading along and come to this big word that I've not learned yet [points to *snowman*], I ask myself if it is made up of words I already know. I'm circling the word *snow* and I'm circling the word *man*. I know both of those words when they are by themselves. So I put the two words together and it says *snowman*."

Scaffolded Assistance

Level 1: Extensive Teacher Help

Say something like:

> "Now let's see if you can do one if I give you some help. In this same sentence on the board, there's another big word we probably don't know [points to *playground*]. I'm going to help you this time by drawing circles around the two parts of the big word [circles *play* and *ground*]. What does the word in the first circle say? Yes, that word is *play*. What does the word in the second circle say? Yes, that word is *ground*. So we know what each of the small words says. Now put them together. Yes, the big word is *playground*. It's a compound word, made up of two smaller words."

Level 2: Less Teacher Help

Say something like:

> "Now let's see if you can figure out what some big words are when I
> give you less help. In the book we will read today, we will find lots
> of new words. One of these is *mussel* [writes it on the board] and
> another is *underwater* [writes it on the board]. Let's see if we can
> use what we know about compound words to figure out these words.
> Look first at this word [points to *mussel*]. That's a word we don't
> know, so we try to figure it out using what we know about compound
> words. What happens when we look at *mussel*? Yes, we can't use
> what we've learned about compound words because it is not made
> up of two little words we know. Now let's look at this word [points
> to *underwater*]. Can we use what we know about compound words?
> Yes. We know the word *under* and we know the word *water* so we
> can put those two words together. What do we get? Yes. The new
> word is *underwater*. So you can see that we can use this strategy
> only when an unknown word is made up of two little words we do
> know."

Level 3: No Teacher Help

The teacher continues doing this exercise, using other compound words,
until she determines the students are ready to move to the *Sea Otter*
book.

Continued Application to Reading

The immediate application of the strategy will occur as the teacher and
the class read *The Sea Otter* together. Each time they encounter an
unknown word, the teacher asks a student (1) "Can we use the compound
word strategy to identify this word?" and (2) "If we can, what are the
two little words, and what is the unknown word?" Continued application
can occur on subsequent days when students read other texts containing
unknown compound words.

POST-LESSON CONSIDERATIONS

Post-Instruction Assessment

You will know students are ready to meet the Common Core standard for morphology if, when they encounter an unknown word in text, they can determine whether the word has structural units and, if so, what the structural units are and what the unknown word is.

Links to Common Core Writing Standards

Understandings about compound words (and other structural units) can be applied to writing as well as reading. When writing their reports as part of the science fair exhibit, students may have need to spell words such as *underwater, shellfish,* and *seaweed.* Integrating into their writing students' understandings from reading about compound words (and other structural units) will strengthen their understanding of how to use structural units to both figure out hard words and to spell hard words.

Example 29

Reading with Expression
(FLUENCY—RF STANDARD 4)

BACKGROUND

Fluency is defined as reading text smoothly and in a manner reflecting the author's meaning. It is a crucial aspect of reading because young readers seldom discover that reading is enjoyable until they experience what it feels like to read text fluently.

Fluency is not to be confused with speed reading. In speed reading, there is no concern about how the reading sounds because the only focus is on how fast a text can be read.

Being a fluent reader means one must know all the words on the page and read the text with proper phrasing and intonation—that is, read it in a manner consistent with the meaning. This example focuses on intonation and phrasing; Example 30 focuses on knowing all the words on the page.

When readers read with intonation and phrasing, they understand what the author was intending to convey, and they say it the way the author intended for it to be said.

To teach intonation and phrasing, first ensure that the students know all the words on the page by sight. Then the readers must use their predicting–monitoring–repredicting skills to anticipate the meaning and to use their background experience to decide what intonation and phrasing is appropriate for that meaning.

The teaching example provided here is based on the Common Core third-grade standard: *Read ... level prose and poetry orally with accuracy, appropriate rate, and expression on successive readings.* It assumes a hypothetical third-grade classroom.

Note to teachers of other grade levels: The suggestions provided here for teaching third graders can be applied with little variation to Common Core fluency standards at other grade levels. For instance, first-grade teachers would use a similar explanation when teaching *RF.1.4b: Read grade-level text orally with accuracy, appropriate rate, and expression on successive readings.*

PRE-LESSON CONSIDERATIONS

Pre-Instruction Assessment

You will know students are not ready to meet the Common Core standard for intonation and phrasing if, despite knowing all the words in the text at sight, they read the text in a monotone or use inappropriate intonation and phrasing that does not reflect the text's meaning.

Large Conceptual Ideas You Can Reinforce during This Lesson

As you teach this lesson, look for opportunities to reinforce big understandings about reading such as the following:

- Authors convey messages having both meaning and feeling.
- Readers must be proactive in doing the predicting–monitoring–repredicting needed to determine the meaning and feeling an author is conveying.
- Reading fluently is not the same as reading fast.
- How one says what is printed in a text is an interpretation, and it should match the author's intended meaning as much as possible.
- Fluency is important because reading is not much fun until you can read text easily.

ORGANIZING FOR INSTRUCTION

Embedding Instruction in Reading for Purpose and Understanding

In this third grade, the class is involved in a poetry-writing project. The teacher has developed the concept of poetry as a form of personal writing in which individuals gain insight into themselves, their thoughts, and their feelings. To aid in developing an understanding of poetry as personal understanding, the teacher has been reading poetry selections from *Salting the Ocean: 100 Poems by Young Poets*, by Naomi Shihab Nye (Greenwillow Books, 2000). She has used these poems as examples of poetry that develop personal insights while also modeling for students appropriate phrasing and intonation. While some students have demonstrated appropriate phrasing and intonation in their reading of the poems, others have not. She now wants to teach intonation and phrasing to the ones who have not yet met the standard to use intonation and phrasing.

Ideas for Differentiating Instruction

One idea you could use if you were this teacher: Students not working with you on this standard work independently at their seats on the poems they are writing or, alternatively, they read poems from one of several books of children's poetry the teacher has supplied.

THE LESSON

Display, Post, or State the Objective

"By the end of this lesson, you will be able to read your own poems, both orally and silently, in ways that communicate the emotion and feeling you wish to convey."

Introducing the Lesson

Say something like:

> "We have been reading a lot of poems from *Salting the Ocean*, and we have seen young poets expressing strong meaning and feelings. And you have been writing your own poems in which you have been trying to convey your own personal feelings. In reading the poems

in *Salting the Ocean*, I have tried to model for you how good readers read poetry in ways that convey the feeling the author intended. If you have a poem you want to share with the class, you will also want to read it in a way that conveys the meaning and feeling you intend. So today I am going to show you how to do this."

Stating the Secret to Doing It

Say something like:

"The secret to doing this is to think first about the feeling you want to convey and to then decide how you would say it to convey that feeling—what parts you would emphasize, what parts you would say loudly, and so on."

Modeling the Thinking

Say something like:

"Let me show you how I do this. Let's start with an example like this sentence:

I don't care what you say.

"If this is a line in my poem, I have to decide how to say it. Depending on what I emphasize with my voice, this sentence can convey six different meanings or feelings, like this:

I don't care what you say.

I *don't* care what you say.

I don't *care* what you say.

I don't care *what* you say.

I don't care what *you* say.

I don't care what you *say.*

"Is it important which way I say it? Yes, because I convey a different meaning when I emphasize different words. Do I mean I don't *care?* Or do I mean that I don't care what *you* say (but that I might care about what someone else says). To decide where to put the emphasis,

I need to decide what meaning I want to convey. Let's say I am writing a poem about getting up on Monday morning to go to school. I think about how I feel about getting up and going to school on Monday mornings. If I love school, and I can't wait to get to school, I would read it so that it sounds cheery and bright. But if I hate getting up on Monday mornings and going to school, I read it in a much more dreary, dragging kind of voice. To be fluent when you read your poems, you have to decide how to say the words to communicate the feeling and meaning you intend."

Scaffolded Assistance

Level 1: Extensive Teacher Help

Say something like:

"Let's do an example together. Let's say I had written this poem:

> The cemetery at midnight
> Was dark and shadowy
> With ghosts flitting here
> And there;
> And I was alone.

"If I am going to read this with a voice that conveys an appropriate meaning, I have to first think about what I know about cemeteries at midnight and the feeling that comes with being out there with the ghosts. Think about your own experiences. How would you feel? Would you read this in a happy, cheery voice? Or with a deeper, more mysterious voice? Yes, you would want to read it in a deeper voice in order to convey the scary idea of being in a cemetery with the ghosts."

Level 2: Less Teacher Help

Say something like:

"Now let's see if you can do one with less help from me. Let's say you were going to read two poems. One is a poem about flowers blooming in the spring and new hope in the world. The other is about the pain and fear of being a soldier in a war. Would you read them both the same way? No. What would you do first? Yes, you would decide what meaning or feeling you wanted to convey. What kind of feeling goes with the poem on flowers? Yes, that is an upbeat meaning. So how would you read it? Yes, in a cheery tone of voice. Would you use the same voice when reading the poem about the soldier? No. You would read it in a voice that conveys sadness, or fear, or pain."

Level 3: No Teacher Help

Say something like:

> "Now try to use what you have learned without any help from me. I am going to show you some short poems from *Salting the Ocean*. Read each poem to yourself, decide what meaning you want to convey, and how you need to say it to convey that feeling. Then you can read it to us and tell us how you decided to read it the way you did."

Continued Application to Reading

What has been learned about intonation and phrasing in this lesson will be applied by the students as they read the poems they have been writing. In addition, the teacher will remind students about reading with intonation and phrasing on other occasions when they are reading orally or silently.

POST-LESSON CONSIDERATIONS

Post-Instruction Assessment

You will know students are ready to meet the Common Core standard for reading with expression if, in oral reading situations, students use intonation and phrasing appropriate to the meaning and feeling expressed in the text.

Links to Common Core Writing Standards

Intonation and phrasing are applicable in writing because good writers give readers clues regarding what intonation and phrasing to use. For instance, a writer might say a character "whined" or "screamed" or that a character was shy or angry. The Common Core writing standards for third grade specify the writing of narratives using "effective technique" (W.3.3), which would include providing the reader with appropriate cues regarding the feeling and meaning intended by the author. Integrating this reading standard with writing helps the development of both reading and writing.

Example 30

Quick Recognition
of Easily Confused Words
(FLUENCY—RF STANDARD 4)

BACKGROUND

While comprehension is a major factor in fluency (see Example 29), fluency also requires quick, accurate recognition of words. Stumbling over words or miscalling words causes a break in fluency; if there are too many breaks, it no longer "sounds like talk."

The most common miscalled words are look-alike words, especially the "glue words" in English such as *then* and *when*, or *that* and *what*. Even though students have previously learned such words by sight, they sometimes say another word that looks like it when reading connected text. They may self-correct the miscue, but too many self-corrections can hinder fluency.

When students confuse look-alike words, it is often because they have not mastered the skill of visually examining words for differences (see also Example 22).

> To teach quick recognition of easily confused words, emphasize the visual differences that distinguish one look-alike word from another.

This teaching example is based on the "accuracy" part of the Common Core's second-grade standard (*RF.2.4b: Read grade-level text orally with accuracy, appropriate rate, and expression on successive readings.* It assumes a hypothetical second-grade classroom.

Note for teachers of other grades: Students at any grade level may confuse look-alike words. The explanation provided in this example can be used at other grade levels with virtually no change. The instructional focus remains on noting differences and on repetition.

PRE-LESSON CONSIDERATIONS

Pre-Instruction Assessment

You will know students are not ready to meet the Common Core standard for accuracy if students frequently miscall similar-looking words (such as saying *there* for *where* or *was* for *saw*).

Large Conceptual Understandings You Can Reinforce during This Lesson

As you teach this lesson, look for opportunities to reinforce big understandings about reading such as the following:

- Word accuracy is important, but comprehension is more important.
- Fluent reading requires knowing words at sight without having to sound them out.

ORGANIZING FOR INSTRUCTION

Embedding Instruction in Reading for Purpose and Understanding

This second-grade class is working on orally reading poetry in fluent, expressive ways for presentation at a local hospital. In previous observations of their reading, the teacher noted that a few students frequently mixed up words such as *there* and *where*. Today she gathers this group of students together to work on those easily confused words. They use as a text "I Met a Man I Could Not See," a poem in John Ciardi's book *I Met a Man* (Houghton Mifflin, 1961). Because the poem contains the words *where* and *there*, the teacher uses this as an occasion to explain how to discriminate among easily confused words so they can read the text smoothly.

Ideas for Differentiating Instruction

One idea you could use if you were this teacher: Students not working with you on this standard are doing USSR (Uninterrupted Sustained Silent Reading) in which students read books of their choice.

THE LESSON

Display, Post, or State the Objective

"By the end of this lesson, you will be able to read a poem and say the look-alike words *where* and *there* quickly and fluently."

Introducing the Lesson

Say something like:

> "I've noticed that you sometimes mix up words that look alike, such as *where* and *there* when reading your poetry. It's hard to tell these apart because they look so much alike. But by the end of today's lesson you will be able to read John Ciardi's 'I Met a Man I Couldn't See' fluently and without any miscalled words, even though it has the words *where* and *there* in it."

Stating the Secret to Doing It

Say something like:

> "The secret to saying easily confused words accurately is to look at what makes these words *different*, not what makes them look alike."

Modeling the Thinking

Say something like:

> "Before we begin reading John Ciardi's poem, let me show you how I quickly recognize these look-alike words. The trick to doing this is to look at how the words are different, not how they are alike. So for these words I say to myself, 'These words look alike because they both end in *-ere*. But the way to tell them apart is to look for what is

different. If there is a *wh* at the beginning, it is *where*; if there is a *th* at the beginning, it is *there*. When I come to these words in a poem, I have to look quickly at what makes them different. If it has a *wh* at the beginning, it is *where*, and if it has *th* at the beginning it is *there*."

Scaffolded Assistance

Level 1: Extensive Teacher Help

Say something like:

> "I'm going to give you some practice on telling these words apart before we move to reading John Ciardi's poem. I have two cards, each with a sentence written on it. One sentence has *where* in it and the other sentence has *there* in it, with the *wh* and the *th* underlined to help you tell them apart. I am going to show the cards to you. What I want you to do is to read the sentence fluently."

Level 2: Less Teacher Help

Say something like:

> "Now I'm going to show you different sentences. One sentence has *where* in it and the other has *there* in it. The words *where* and *there* do not have the *wh* and *th* underlined in these sentences. I want you to read the two sentences fluently, without hesitating over the words *where* or *there*."

Level 3: No Teacher Help

Say something like:

> "Okay, now I'm going to make it harder. I have put both *where* and *there* in each sentence. When I show you the sentence, read it fluently without stumbling over either *where* or *there*."

Continued Application to Reading

The immediate application of this lesson will occur when the students read Ciardi's poem "I Met a Man I Could Not See." Ultimately, this skill will be applied when they present their poems at the hospital. Subsequently, the teacher will use this lesson as a springboard for eliminating confusion over other look-alike words.

POST-LESSON CONSIDERATIONS

Post-Instruction Assessment

You will know students are ready to meet the Common Core standard for accuracy when they accurately and quickly say easily confused words when reading text.

Links to Common Core Writing Standards

The more students use easily confused words in their writing, the more likely it is that they will not confuse the words when they encounter them in print. Therefore, when completing Common Core writing standards, students should be encouraged to use words that they tend to confuse when they are reading.

Appendix

Research Foundations
for This Book

The third edition of *Explaining Reading* is based on research in explicit teaching, authentic literacy tasks, and adaptive teaching. The following books and journal articles are my primary sources.

RESEARCH ON EXPLICIT TEACHING

Almasi, J., & Hart, S. (2011). Best practices in comprehension instruction. In L. M. Morrow & L. B. Gambrell (Eds.), *Best practices in literacy instruction* (4th ed., pp. 250–275). New York: Guilford Press.

Archer, A., & Hughes, C. (2010). *Explicit instruction: Effective and efficient teaching.* New York: Guilford Press.

Block, C., & Duffy, G. (2008). Research on teaching comprehension. In C. Block & S. R. Paris (Eds.) *Comprehension instruction: Research-based best practices* (pp. 19–37). New York: Guilford Press.

Dole, J., Brown, K., & Trathen, W. (1996). The effects of strategy instruction on the comprehension of at-risk students. *Reading Research Quarterly, 31,* 62–89.

Duffy, G., Miller, S., Howerton, S. & Williams, J. (2010). Comprehension instruction: Merging two historically antithetical perspectives. In D. Wyse, R. Andrews, & J. Hoffman (Eds.), *The Routledge international handbook of English, language and literacy teaching* (pp. 58–73). New York: Routledge.

Duffy, G., Roehler, L., Sivan, E., Rackliffe, G., Book, C., Meloth, M., et al. (1987). Effects of explaining the reasoning associated with using reading strategies. *Reading Research Quarterly, 22,* 347–368.

Many, J. (2002). An exhibition and analysis of verbal tapestries: Understanding how scaffolding is woven into the fabric of instructional conversations. *Reading Research Quarterly, 37* (4), 376–407.

Pressley, M., El-Dinary, P., Gaskins, I., Schuder, T., Bergman, J., Almasi, L., et al. (1992). Beyond direct explanation: Transactional instruction of reading comprehension strategies. *Elementary School Journal, 92*, 511–554.

AUTHENTIC LITERACY TASKS

Brophy. J. (2008). Developing students' appreciation for what is taught in school. *Educational Psychologist, 43*(3), 132–411.

Duffy, G. (1997). Powerful models or powerful teachers? An argument for teachers-as-entrepreneurs. In St. Stahl & D. Hayes (Eds.), *Instructional models in reading* (pp. 351–367). Mahwah, NJ: Lawrence Erlbaum.

Fisher, C., & Hiebert, E. (1990). Characteristics of tasks in two approaches to literacy instruction. *Elementary School Journal, 91*(1), 3–18.

Gee, J. (2004). *Situated language and learning: A critique of traditional schooling.* New York: Routledge.

Miller, S. (2003). How high- and low-challenge tasks affect motivation and learning: Implications for struggling readers. *Reading and Writing Quarterly, 19*, 39–57.

Parsons, S. (2008). Providing all students ACCESS to self-regulated literacy learning. *The Reading Teacher, 61*, 628–635.

Parsons, S., Metzger, S., Askew, J., & Carswell, A. (2011). Teaching against the grain: One Title I school's journey toward project-based literacy instruction. *Literacy Research and Instruction, 50*(1), 1–14.

Purcell-Gates, V., Duke, N., & Martineau, J. (2007). Learning to read and write genre-specific text: Roles of authentic experience and explicit teaching. *Reading Research Quarterly, 42*(1), 8–35.

ADAPTIVE TEACHING

Allen, M., Matthews, C., & Parsons, S. (2013). A second-grade teacher's adaptive teaching during an integrated science-literacy unit. *Teaching and Teacher Education, 35*, 114–125.

Corno, L. (2008). On teaching adaptively. *Educational Psychologist, 43*, 161–173.

Duffy, G. (2005). Metacognition and the development of reading teachers. In C. Block, S. Israel, K. Kinnucan-Welsch, & K. Bauserman (Eds.), *Metacognition and literacy learning* (pp. 299–314). Mahwah, NJ: Erlbaum.

Duffy, G., Miller, S., Parsons, S., & Meloth, M. (2009). Teachers as metacognitive professionals. In D. Hacker, J. Dunlosky, & A. Graesser (Eds.), *Handbook of metacognition in education* (pp. 240–256). New York: Routledge.

Fairbanks, C., Duffy, G., Faircloth, B., He, Y., Levin, B., Rohr, et al. (2010). Beyond knowledge: Exploring why some teachers are more thoughtfully adaptive than others. *Journal of Teacher Education, 61*, 161–171.

Parsons, S. (2012). Adaptive teaching in literacy instruction: Case studies of two teachers. *Journal of Literacy Research, 44*(2), 149–170.

Roehler, L., Duffy, G., & Warren, S. (1988). Adaptive explanatory actions associated with teaching of reading strategies. In J. Readance & S. Baldwin (Eds.), The 37th *Yearbook of the National Reading Conference: Dialogues in literacy research* (pp. 339–346). Chicago: National Reading Conference.

Sawyer, R. (2004). Creative teaching: Collaborative improvisation. *Educational Researcher, 33*(2), 12–20.

Index